Contents

Using Bite Times 4
Moon Phases 5
Bite Time Adjustments 7
Fremantle Tide Times .... 8 - 39
Bite Times .... 40 - 69
Exmouth Tide Times .... 70 - 101
Fish ID 102

Fish Illustrations: Trevor Hawkins

Published in 2025 by
Australian Fishing Network Pty Ltd
PO Box 544, Croydon, VIC 3136
Tel: (03) 9729 8788 Email: sales@afn.com.au www.afn.com.au

 ISBN 9781 8651 3438 3

DISCLAIMER

The solar/lunar bite times in this book were derived from the program* WXTide32 *and are predictions. While they are as accurate as possible, they should be used as a guide only. Local conditions and changes can cause variations, so consult a website such as the* Bureau of Meteorology Oceanographic Services, (www.bom.gov.au/oceanography/tides) *as close as possible to the tide date and time before your fishing trip for the most up-to-date information and if you require certified information.
The publisher, Australian Fishing Network, advises that the information in this guide should not be used for navigation and should not be relied on for crucial situations.

"This product is based on Bureau of Meteorology information that has subsequently been modified. The Bureau does not necessarily support or endorse, or have any connection with, the product.
In respect of that part of the information which is sourced from the Bureau, and to the maximum extent permitted by law:
(i) The Bureau makes no representation and gives no warranty of any kind whether express, implied, statutory or otherwise in respect to the availability, accuracy, currency, completeness, quality or reliability of the information or that the information will be fit for any particular purpose or will not infringe any third party Intellectual Property rights; and
(ii) the Bureau's liability for any loss, damage, cost or expense resulting from use of, or reliance on, the information is entirely excluded."
"The Bureau of Meteorology gives no warranty of any kind whether express, implied, statutory or otherwise in respect to the availability, accuracy, currency, completeness, quality or reliability of the information or that the information will be fit for any particular purpose or will not infringe any third party Intellectual Property rights. The Bureau's liability for any loss, damage, cost or expense resulting from use of, or reliance on, the information is entirely excluded."

Tim Smith's

Using Bite Times

'Solunar' theory suggests all creatures great and small respond in some way to the influences of both the Sun and the Moon during the course of a day.

This book lists the peak activity times along with the moon phases and it should become an indispensable tool for when you're planning a trip.
The peak activity times are presented in this book to simulate the logical progression of the Moon as it orbits the Earth. The first is the minor peak at moonrise, no matter what time of day at which it occurs. The second is the major peak when the moon is directly overhead, the third is the minor peak at moonset and the fourth is the major peak when the moon is directly overhead on the opposite side of the globe.

Solunar (solar and lunar) theory is one of nature's mysteries which many of us find difficult to consider with any merit. A number of books, tables and articles have been written on the subject of lunar and solar influences on animal behaviour. Solunar theory suggests all creatures great and small respond in some way to the influences of both the Sun and the Moon during the course of a day. Specifically this response is often seen as an increase or decrease in activity level. Increased activity periods have often been referred to as peak or prime times.
The combination of centrifugal force produced by the Earth's rotation and the Moon's daily crossing of the sky generates our tides. Such enormous force is produced by these phenomena that it causes the Earth's surface to bulge up to 16 centimetres. Could lunar cycles impact on man? You be the judge. The human gestation period is 266 days, the average synodic interval between two consecutive new Moons is 29.530589 days; 266 divided by 29.530589 equals 9.008 lunar months. Sound familiar? Man is made up of approximately 80 per cent water. We know what happens tidally to huge bodies of water. Do you think there is a remote possibility that we too could unknowingly experience the effects of this heavenly sphere?

It is important to understand that what influences one creature may not influence another in any circumstance. For example there are a number of intertidal organisms that are most active when submerged by an incoming tide, creatures such as barnacles, green crabs, snails, clams, and oysters. Others, like soldier crabs and shorebirds, are especially adapted to feed on beaches exposed at low tide. The lower the creature's order in the animal kingdom the more likely it is to respond to solar and lunar stimuli.

LIGHT THEORY

The light theory suggests that light levels during the day and night dictate feeding activity times. For example it is said that fishing is better on the mornings immediately leading up to and following the period of new Moon because the fish have been unable to feed during the periods of low light during the night. Fishing is also said to be good during the nights leading up to and following the full Moon because of increased evening light levels.

SOLAR THEORY

To some extent the solar theory is reliant upon seasonal changes, therefore I have provided you with a brief summary of the seasonal patterns and how they influence the Southern Hemisphere.

The principle of the solar theory works on the various instances of the Sun's rise, upper transit, set, and lower transit to identify the peak activity periods. Following a long period of darkness the animal kingdom is given a kick-start to the day as dawn approaches. Many creatures stir from their rest period and warm with the Sun to commence the daily routine of food gathering. All animal life has a preferred temperature range and fish are no exception to this rule. It is said that seasonal conditions may dictate when particular fish species will commence to feed.

So although dawn and dusk have been historically noted as prime fishing times if we review the seasonal fluctuations in day and night time temperatures we may see cause for reassessing our reliance on these times. For example during the colder months peak feeding times may coincide during the warmest time of the day; just after midday when the water temperatures have increased to a more preferred level. Conversely, during the warmer months peak feeding times may align with the coolest times of the day; dusk 'til dawn.

SEASONS

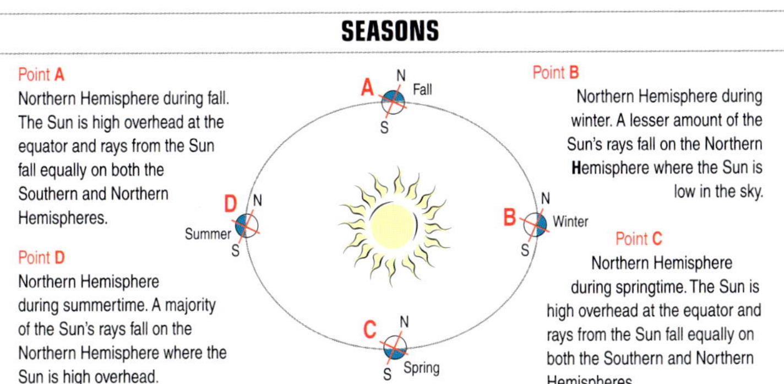

LUNAR THEORY

To help you understand the lunar theory in more depth I have provided a brief outline of the various lunar phases. When you watch the Moon over a course of several days you will see that its appearance changes. The varying appearances called 'phases' depend upon the relative positions of the Sun and Moon.

MOON PHASES

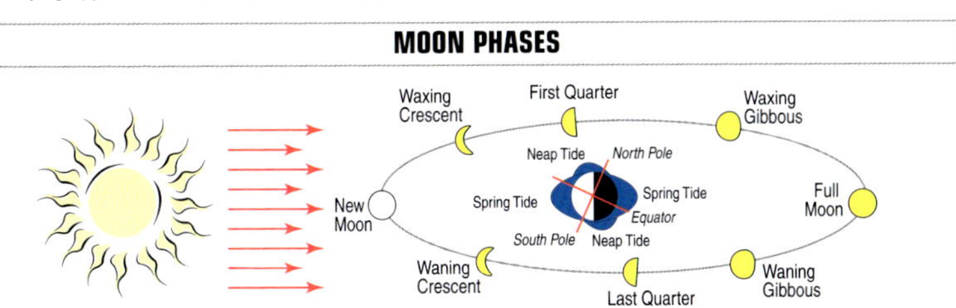

NEW MOON

When the Moon is between the Sun and the Earth we cannot see any of the illuminated side of the Moon, the Moon is dark, we call this phase the new Moon and it is the beginning of a new lunar month. The Moon rises and sets with the Sun during the new Moon. The gravitational forces exerted on the Earth by the Moon and the Sun is greatest at this time. The first of the spring tides for the lunar month occurs during this period.

FIRST QUARTER

The amount of lighted surface visible from the Earth begins to grow and we see a waxing crescent Moon. When the Moon reaches the first quarter we see half of it lit. The Moon rises during the middle of the day and is overhead about dusk and sets around midnight. The Moon's illuminated side will appear on the right in the Northern Hemisphere. The gravitational forces on the Earth have reduced since the new Moon and now the combined pull of the Moon and the Sun is at a minimum for the lunar month. The first of the neap tides for the Lunar month occurs at this time.

FULL MOON

As the illuminated portion grows we have a waxing gibbous Moon. The full Moon occurs when the Moon reaches the side of the Earth opposite from the Sun. It appears large and bright. The Moon rises as the Sun is setting—it is overhead about midnight and sets close to dawn. The gravitational forces on the Earth have increased since the first quarter and now the combined pull of the Moon and the Sun is at a maximum again for the lunar month, the second of the spring tides occur.

LAST QUARTER

The gravitational forces on the Earth have reduced since the full Moon and now the combined pull of the Moon and the Sun is at a minimum again for the lunar month. The second of the neap tides for the lunar month occurs at this time. As a waning crescent, the Moon diminishes to a thin sliver, returning to a new Moon after approximately 29.5 solar days or one lunar month. As the Moon revolves around the Earth it rotates on its own axis at the same rate it revolves, therefore the Moon always keeps the same face toward the Earth.

TIDAL FORCES

As the Earth rotates on its axis once every 24 hours relative to the Sun, and 24 hours and 53 minutes relative to the Moon; the Moon rises approximately 53 minutes later with respect to the Sun each day. This delay or lagging can be seen in the variation of tides from day to day.

The principle of the lunar theory works on the various instances of the Moon's rise, upper transit, set, and lower transit to identify the peak activity periods. This theory can also take into account the various lunar phases and the proximity (apogee and perigee) of the Moon to the Earth during the period of one lunation (new Moon to new Moon). Because the Moon orbits the Earth on an elliptical path, the distance between the two is always changing. The Moon has less gravitational influence on the Earth around the time of apogee when the distance between the two bodies is at a maximum. Greater gravitational influence occurs around the time of perigee when the distance between the Earth and the Moon is at a minimum.

SOLUNAR THEORY

Solunar theory accounts for the peaks associated with both the solar and lunar theories. It also incorporates the Sun's lower transit (midnight), and it also flags the coinciding times of peaks from the other theories. In other words it takes an each way bet on the three individual theories. Additionally the solunar theory recognises the gravitational effect on the Earth from the combined force produced by the Moon and the Sun in tandem. This gravitational force changes with the seasons, with the phases of the Moon, and with the Sun and Moon's proximity to Earth.

EFFECTS ON FISHING

Fishing wise, catch rates are often said to be higher around the new and full Moon phases. This makes sense when you consider the increased gravitational influence on the Earth during these periods. However this is further bolstered if you consider that during these times we are provided with three windows of peak activity level during general daylight hours, each coinciding with dawn, noon, or dusk. Around the period of new Moon, the Moon is in harmony with the Sun, they rise, transit and set together. During the period of full Moon, the Moon and Sun directly oppose each other, the Moon sets when the Sun rises, the Moon is underfoot at noon, and the Moon rises at Sun set. Whether or not the increased activity levels in lower organisms is the catalyst for larger and perhaps predatory creatures to begin feeding is arguable. Your observations will also show increased activity levels in the non predatory herbivore family during the peak times.

FEEDING PATTERNS

Does activity occur outside of these peak periods? Of course. Remember not all species will react in an identical manner during the peak times. The bottom line is fish don't always feel hungry! They follow certain feeding patterns but aren't totally immune to sampling the odd tid-bit throughout the course of the day. As with most creatures, strength is gained through struggle; and only the fittest and strongest survive in the wild. While minimum work for maximum return is the hallmark of big fish, a fish's condition and health must also be maintained through foraging for food. Natural rhythms aside, fish are also subject to local conditions such as the various fluctuations in air temperature, barometric pressure, water levels, water clarity, and water temperature. These should all be considered when using the tables.

BITE TIME ADJUSTMENTS (Minutes)

Approximate variation times only, taken from various sources.

Location	Minutes
Albany	-10
Augusta	0
Broome	-30
Busselton	0
Carnarvon	+10
Dampier	-5
Derby	-30
Esperance	-20
Eucla	-50
Exmouth	+5
Gearaldton	+5
Geraldton	+10
Jurien	+5
Kalbarri	+5
Kalgoolie	-20
Kununurra	-50
Mandurah	0
Onslow	0
Pemberton	0
Perth	0
Port Hedland	-10
Rottnest Island	0
Shark Bay	+10
Steep Point	+10
Wyndham	-50

POPULAR TIDE ADJUSTMENTS

Cervantes	-2min
Hillarys	-15min
Lancelin	0
Rottnest Island	-10min
Swan River Causeway	+1hr
Two Rocks Marina	-10min
Warnbro Sound	-10min
Bunbury	- 15min
Busselton	- 22min
Canning Bridge	+ 1hr 20min
Mandurah	- 2min
Peel Inlet	+ 3hr
Rockingham	+ 6min
Warnbro Sound	- 12min
Geraldton	- 30min
Kalbarri	- 30min

Fremantle

Day	Date		Tide 1
Mon	1		1:33 AM (1.02) **H**
Tue	2		4:15 AM (1.02) **H**
Wed	3		5:43 AM (1.05) **H**
Thu	4		6:58 AM (1.08) **H**
Fri	5		7:46 AM (1.11) **H**
Sat	6		12:45 AM (0.77) L
Sun	7		1:52 AM (0.73) L
Mon	8	○	2:49 AM (0.70) L
Tue	9		3:54 AM (0.68) L
Wed	10		5:09 AM (0.66) L
Thu	11		6:27 AM (0.66) L
Fri	12		9:52 AM (0.61) L
Sat	13		1:02 PM (0.52) L
Sun	14		12:10 AM (1.07) **H**
Mon	15		12:45 AM (1.04) **H**
Tue	16		4:04 AM (1.03) **H**
Wed	17		6:29 AM (1.02) **H**
Thu	18		7:30 AM (1.02) **H**
Fri	19		12:09 AM (0.77) L
Sat	20		1:45 AM (0.73) L
Sun	21		3:00 AM (0.70) L
Mon	22	●	3:45 AM (0.68) L
Tue	23		4:20 AM (0.66) L
Wed	24		4:56 AM (0.64) L
Thu	25		5:34 AM (0.63) L
Fri	26		6:16 AM (0.63) L
Sat	27		9:49 AM (0.62) L
Sun	28		10:57 AM (0.60) L
Mon	29		12:02 AM (1.02) **H**
Tue	30		12:38 AM (1.00) **H**

Tide 2	Tide 3	Tide 4
3:02 PM (0.59) L		
3:25 PM (0.56) L		
3:46 PM (0.54) L		
4:03 PM (0.53) L		
4:16 PM (0.54) L	11:35 PM (0.77) **H**	
8:30 AM (1.12) **H**	4:30 PM (0.56) L	10:50 PM (0.78) **H**
9:13 AM (1.09) **H**	4:45 PM (0.60) L	10:57 PM (0.82) **H**
9:59 AM (1.03) **H**	4:56 PM (0.65) L	11:15 PM (0.87) **H**
11:07 AM (0.94) **H**	4:47 PM (0.70) L	11:32 PM (0.93) **H**
12:25 PM (0.84) **H**	4:12 PM (0.72) L	11:14 PM (0.99) **H**
1:28 PM (0.73) **H**	3:53 PM (0.70) L	11:20 PM (1.04) **H**
10:47 AM (0.61) L	12:17 PM (0.60) L	11:42 PM (1.07) **H**
1:45 PM (0.47) L		
1:43 AM (1.04) L	3:00 AM (1.05) **H**	2:26 PM (0.45) L
3:04 PM (0.46) L		
3:38 PM (0.50) L		
4:02 PM (0.54) L	11:53 PM (0.77) **H**	
8:13 AM (1.01) **H**	3:59 PM (0.60) L	10:19 PM (0.78) **H**
8:50 AM (0.98) **H**	3:54 PM (0.64) L	10:20 PM (0.82) **H**
9:25 AM (0.94) **H**	3:55 PM (0.67) L	10:18 PM (0.86) **H**
9:58 AM (0.89) **H**	3:19 PM (0.69) L	10:01 PM (0.91) **H**
10:30 AM (0.83) **H**	3:18 PM (0.68) L	9:59 PM (0.96) **H**
10:42 AM (0.77) **H**	3:31 PM (0.68) L	10:14 PM (1.00) **H**
10:44 AM (0.71) **H**	3:31 PM (0.67) L	10:36 PM (1.03) **H**
10:58 AM (0.67) **H**	2:59 PM (0.65) L	11:02 PM (1.04) **H**
11:13 AM (0.63) **H**	12:45 PM (0.62) L	11:31 PM (1.04) **H**
11:11 AM (0.60) L	1:15 PM (0.58) L	
1:45 PM (0.56) L		
2:11 PM (0.54) L		

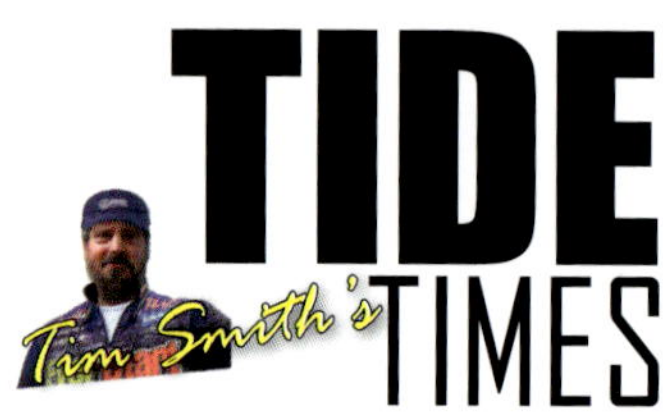

POPULAR TIDE ADJUSTMENTS

Cervantes	-2min
Hillarys	-15min
Lancelin	0
Rottnest Island	-10min
Swan River Causeway	+1hr
Two Rocks Marina	-10min
Warnbro Sound	-10min
Bunbury	- 15min
Busselton	- 22min
Canning Bridge	+ 1hr 20min
Mandurah	- 2min
Peel Inlet	+ 3hr
Rockingham	+ 6min
Warnbro Sound	- 12min
Geraldton	- 30min
Kalbarri	- 30min

Fremantle

Day	Date	Tide 1
Wed	1	1:26 AM (0.97) **H**
Thu	2	4:42 AM (0.96) **H**
Fri	3	6:24 AM (0.98) **H**
Sat	4	12:28 AM (0.78) L
Sun	5	1:37 AM (0.72) L
Mon	6	2:52 AM (0.66) L
Tue	7 ○	4:00 AM (0.59) L
Wed	8	5:01 AM (0.54) L
Thu	9	6:30 AM (0.51) L
Fri	10	8:29 AM (0.47) L
Sat	11	9:45 AM (0.45) L
Sun	12	12:27 PM (0.42) L
Mon	13	1:13 PM (0.42) L
Tue	14	12:06 AM (1.00) **H**
Wed	15	12:43 AM (0.93) **H**
Thu	16	6:15 AM (0.89) **H**
Fri	17	12:41 AM (0.78) L
Sat	18	2:14 AM (0.73) L
Sun	19	2:58 AM (0.68) L
Mon	20	3:37 AM (0.63) L
Tue	21 ●	4:15 AM (0.59) L
Wed	22	4:52 AM (0.56) L
Thu	23	5:30 AM (0.54) L
Fri	24	6:17 AM (0.53) L
Sat	25	8:17 AM (0.52) L
Sun	26	9:07 AM (0.53) L
Mon	27	9:56 AM (0.54) L
Tue	28	10:55 AM (0.55) L
Wed	29	12:04 AM (1.00) **H**
Thu	30	12:45 AM (0.96) **H**
Fri	31	3:28 AM (0.91) **H**

Tide 2	Tide 3	Tide 4
2:33 PM (0.53) L		
2:50 PM (0.53) L		
3:00 PM (0.54) L	10:27 PM (0.79) **H**	
7:30 AM (0.99) **H**	3:09 PM (0.57) L	9:23 PM (0.81) **H**
8:26 AM (0.97) **H**	3:19 PM (0.61) L	9:23 PM (0.86) **H**
9:32 AM (0.92) **H**	3:24 PM (0.66) L	9:31 PM (0.93) **H**
10:48 AM (0.85) **H**	3:01 PM (0.70) L	9:40 PM (1.00) **H**
11:53 AM (0.77) **H**	2:40 PM (0.71) L	9:54 PM (1.06) **H**
1:00 PM (0.68) **H**	2:13 PM (0.68) L	10:14 PM (1.11) **H**
10:38 PM (1.12) **H**		
10:23 AM (0.45) L	11:30 AM (0.45) L	11:04 PM (1.11) **H**
11:34 PM (1.06) **H**		
1:34 AM (0.98) L	2:27 AM (0.99) **H**	1:53 PM (0.46) L
1:52 AM (0.92) L	3:29 AM (0.94) **H**	2:27 PM (0.51) L
2:49 PM (0.57) L	10:16 PM (0.80) **H**	
7:18 AM (0.87) **H**	2:44 PM (0.63) L	8:57 PM (0.83) **H**
8:11 AM (0.85) **H**	2:29 PM (0.66) L	8:52 PM (0.88) **H**
9:05 AM (0.82) **H**	2:13 PM (0.69) L	8:43 PM (0.93) **H**
9:59 AM (0.79) **H**	1:41 PM (0.69) L	8:43 PM (0.98) **H**
10:47 AM (0.75) **H**	1:56 PM (0.68) L	8:54 PM (1.03) **H**
11:32 AM (0.72) **H**	2:12 PM (0.68) L	9:12 PM (1.06) **H**
12:18 PM (0.68) **H**	2:12 PM (0.67) L	9:34 PM (1.08) **H**
10:00 PM (1.09) **H**		
10:28 PM (1.08) **H**		
10:58 PM (1.06) **H**		
11:46 AM (0.55) **H**	12:03 PM (0.55) L	11:29 PM (1.03) **H**
11:34 AM (0.55) L	12:48 PM (0.54) L	
1:16 PM (0.54) L		
1:34 PM (0.55) L		
1:34 PM (0.57) L	9:38 PM (0.83) **H**	11:56 PM (0.82) L

POPULAR TIDE ADJUSTMENTS

Cervantes	-2min
Hillarys	-15min
Lancelin	0
Rottnest Island	-10min
Swan River Causeway	+1hr
Two Rocks Marina	-10min
Warnbro Sound	-10min
Bunbury	- 15min
Busselton	- 22min
Canning Bridge	+ 1hr 20min
Mandurah	- 2min
Peel Inlet	+ 3hr
Rockingham	+ 6min
Warnbro Sound	- 12min
Geraldton	- 30min
Kalbarri	- 30min

Fremantle

Day	Date	Tide 1
Sat	1	5:15 AM (0.88) **H**
Sun	2	1:17 AM (0.74) L
Mon	3	2:39 AM (0.65) L
Tue	4	3:41 AM (0.55) L
Wed	5	4:45 AM (0.47) L
Thu	6 ○	6:10 AM (0.40) L
Fri	7	7:22 AM (0.36) L
Sat	8	8:20 AM (0.35) L
Sun	9	9:25 AM (0.39) L
Mon	10	11:46 AM (0.42) L
Tue	11	12:37 PM (0.47) L
Wed	12	1:16 PM (0.54) L
Thu	13	1:44 PM (0.61) L
Fri	14	1:17 PM (0.68) L
Sat	15	5:34 AM (0.73) L
Sun	16	4:26 AM (0.68) L
Mon	17	4:41 AM (0.62) L
Tue	18	4:26 AM (0.57) L
Wed	19	4:59 AM (0.52) L
Thu	20 ●	5:41 AM (0.48) L
Fri	21	6:23 AM (0.46) L
Sat	22	7:05 AM (0.45) L
Sun	23	7:45 AM (0.46) L
Mon	24	8:25 AM (0.48) L
Tue	25	9:06 AM (0.50) L
Wed	26	9:46 AM (0.53) L
Thu	27	10:26 AM (0.57) L
Fri	28	12:14 AM (0.95) **H**
Sat	29	12:44 AM (0.88) **H**
Sun	30	11:35 AM (0.69) L

NOVEMBER 2025

Tide 2	Tide 3	Tide 4
1:34 PM (0.60) L	8:05 PM (0.86) **H**	
7:15 AM (0.84) **H**	1:41 PM (0.65) L	8:01 PM (0.93) **H**
9:00 AM (0.81) **H**	1:44 PM (0.69) L	8:11 PM (1.01) **H**
10:22 AM (0.77) **H**	1:27 PM (0.72) L	8:29 PM (1.08) **H**
11:31 AM (0.72) **H**	12:51 PM (0.72) L	8:51 PM (1.15) **H**
9:16 PM (1.19) **H**		
9:45 PM (1.20) **H**		
10:13 PM (1.17) **H**		
10:40 PM (1.11) **H**		
11:06 PM (1.04) **H**		
11:33 PM (0.96) **H**		
9:57 PM (0.88) **H**	10:10 PM (0.88) L	11:57 PM (0.89) **H**
9:30 PM (0.85) **H**		
7:51 PM (0.88) **H**		
6:33 AM (0.73) L	12:20 PM (0.70) L	7:44 PM (0.93) **H**
9:05 AM (0.71) **H**	11:07 AM (0.70) L	7:41 PM (0.99) **H**
10:06 AM (0.71) **H**	11:37 AM (0.70) L	7:45 PM (1.04) **H**
10:56 AM (0.70) **H**	12:07 PM (0.70) L	7:59 PM (1.09) **H**
11:54 AM (0.69) **H**	12:22 PM (0.69) L	8:17 PM (1.12) **H**
8:40 PM (1.14) **H**		
9:07 PM (1.15) **H**		
9:36 PM (1.14) **H**		
10:06 PM (1.12) **H**		
10:36 PM (1.09) **H**		
11:08 PM (1.05) **H**		
11:41 PM (1.01) **H**		
11:00 AM (0.60) L	9:42 PM (0.88) **H**	11:14 PM (0.87) L
11:25 AM (0.64) L	7:05 PM (0.90) **H**	
6:55 PM (0.97) **H**		

POPULAR TIDE ADJUSTMENTS

Cervantes	-2min
Hillarys	-15min
Lancelin	0
Rottnest Island	-10min
Swan River Causeway	+1hr
Two Rocks Marina	-10min
Warnbro Sound	-10min
Bunbury	- 15min
Busselton	- 22min
Canning Bridge	+ 1hr 20min
Mandurah	- 2min
Peel Inlet	+ 3hr
Rockingham	+ 6min
Warnbro Sound	- 12min
Geraldton	- 30min
Kalbarri	- 30min

Fremantle

Day	Date		Tide 1	
Mon	1		3:35 AM	(0.67) L
Tue	2		4:09 AM	(0.55) L
Wed	3		4:56 AM	(0.44) L
Thu	4		5:45 AM	(0.35) L
Fri	5	○	6:32 AM	(0.30) L
Sat	6		7:19 AM	(0.30) L
Sun	7		8:05 AM	(0.33) L
Mon	8		8:50 AM	(0.40) L
Tue	9		9:30 AM	(0.48) L
Wed	10		9:47 AM	(0.57) L
Thu	11		9:52 AM	(0.64) L
Fri	12		7:38 AM	(0.65) L
Sat	13		7:38 AM	(0.64) L
Sun	14		6:51 AM	(0.62) L
Mon	15		5:35 AM	(0.59) L
Tue	16		5:14 AM	(0.55) L
Wed	17		5:21 AM	(0.50) L
Thu	18		5:33 AM	(0.46) L
Fri	19		5:54 AM	(0.44) L
Sat	20	●	6:20 AM	(0.42) L
Sun	21		6:49 AM	(0.42) L
Mon	22		7:16 AM	(0.44) L
Tue	23		7:41 AM	(0.47) L
Wed	24		7:58 AM	(0.50) L
Thu	25		8:03 AM	(0.54) L
Fri	26		8:00 AM	(0.58) L
Sat	27		7:51 AM	(0.62) L
Sun	28		7:40 AM	(0.64) L
Mon	29		6:25 AM	(0.63) L
Tue	30		4:07 AM	(0.54) L
Wed	31		4:32 AM	(0.44) L

Tide 2	Tide 3	Tide 4
7:03 PM (1.05) **H**		
7:25 PM (1.14) **H**		
7:54 PM (1.21) **H**		
8:27 PM (1.25) **H**		
9:02 PM (1.25) **H**		
9:38 PM (1.22) **H**		
10:09 PM (1.17) **H**		
10:30 PM (1.09) **H**		
10:45 PM (1.01) **H**		
11:00 PM (0.94) **H**		
9:04 PM (0.89) **H**		
7:11 PM (0.89) **H**		
6:45 PM (0.95) **H**		
6:46 PM (1.01) **H**		
6:53 PM (1.06) **H**		
7:08 PM (1.11) **H**		
7:30 PM (1.14) **H**		
7:55 PM (1.16) **H**		
8:25 PM (1.17) **H**		
8:57 PM (1.17) **H**		
9:30 PM (1.16) **H**		
10:01 PM (1.14) **H**		
10:31 PM (1.10) **H**		
11:00 PM (1.05) **H**		
11:26 PM (0.99) **H**		
11:45 PM (0.91) **H**		
5:57 PM (0.89) **H**		
5:35 PM (0.96) **H**		
5:45 PM (1.05) **H**		
6:17 PM (1.13) **H**		
6:57 PM (1.20) **H**		

POPULAR TIDE ADJUSTMENTS

Cervantes	-2min
Hillarys	-15min
Lancelin	0
Rottnest Island	-10min
Swan River Causeway	+1hr
Two Rocks Marina	-10min
Warnbro Sound	-10min
Bunbury	- 15min
Busselton	- 22min
Canning Bridge	+ 1hr 20min
Mandurah	- 2min
Peel Inlet	+ 3hr
Rockingham	+ 6min
Warnbro Sound	- 12min
Geraldton	- 30min
Kalbarri	- 30min

Fremantle

Day	Date	Tide 1
Thu	1	5:09 AM (0.36) L
Fri	2	5:48 AM (0.31) L
Sat	3 ○	6:29 AM (0.30) L
Sun	4	7:07 AM (0.33) L
Mon	5	7:41 AM (0.39) L
Tue	6	8:02 AM (0.47) L
Wed	7	8:04 AM (0.56) L
Thu	8	7:08 AM (0.61) L
Fri	9	6:36 AM (0.61) L
Sat	10	6:38 AM (0.60) L
Sun	11	6:30 AM (0.58) L
Mon	12	5:52 AM (0.57) L
Tue	13	5:28 AM (0.54) L
Wed	14	5:00 AM (0.51) L
Thu	15	5:06 AM (0.48) L
Fri	16	5:21 AM (0.45) L
Sat	17	5:42 AM (0.44) L
Sun	18	6:03 AM (0.43) L
Mon	19 ●	6:21 AM (0.44) L
Tue	20	6:34 AM (0.47) L
Wed	21	6:44 AM (0.50) L
Thu	22	6:49 AM (0.54) L
Fri	23	6:48 AM (0.58) L
Sat	24	6:38 AM (0.61) L
Sun	25	6:28 AM (0.62) L
Mon	26	5:37 AM (0.60) L
Tue	27	5:00 AM (0.55) L
Wed	28	3:48 AM (0.46) L
Thu	29	4:20 AM (0.39) L
Fri	30	4:57 AM (0.35) L
Sat	31	5:34 AM (0.35) L

JANUARY 2026

Tide 2	Tide 3	Tide 4
7:39 PM (1.25) **H**		
8:24 PM (1.27) **H**		
9:09 PM (1.25) **H**		
9:53 PM (1.21) **H**		
10:29 PM (1.13) **H**		
10:37 PM (1.05) **H**		
10:31 PM (0.97) **H**		
10:21 PM (0.90) **H**		
8:37 PM (0.88) **H**		
5:18 PM (0.92) **H**		
5:23 PM (0.98) **H**		
5:40 PM (1.03) **H**		
6:07 PM (1.07) **H**		
6:38 PM (1.11) **H**		
7:12 PM (1.14) **H**		
7:46 PM (1.16) **H**		
8:22 PM (1.18) **H**		
8:58 PM (1.18) **H**		
9:31 PM (1.16) **H**		
10:03 PM (1.13) **H**		
1:28 PM (0.74) **H**	3:03 PM (0.74) L	10:31 PM (1.07) **H**
1:44 PM (0.78) **H**	4:01 PM (0.76) L	10:56 PM (1.00) **H**
2:10 PM (0.83) **H**	5:07 PM (0.80) L	11:15 PM (0.91) **H**
2:40 PM (0.89) **H**	6:59 PM (0.83) L	8:49 PM (0.84) **H**
3:15 PM (0.96) **H**		
3:56 PM (1.03) **H**		
4:45 PM (1.09) **H**		
5:43 PM (1.15) **H**		
6:44 PM (1.20) **H**		
7:41 PM (1.23) **H**		
8:31 PM (1.23) **H**		

POPULAR TIDE ADJUSTMENTS

Cervantes	-2min
Hillarys	-15min
Lancelin	0
Rottnest Island	-10min
Swan River Causeway	+1hr
Two Rocks Marina	-10min
Warnbro Sound	-10min
Bunbury	- 15min
Busselton	- 22min
Canning Bridge	+ 1hr 20min
Mandurah	- 2min
Peel Inlet	+ 3hr
Rockingham	+ 6min
Warnbro Sound	- 12min
Geraldton	- 30min
Kalbarri	- 30min

Fremantle

Day	Date	Tide 1
Sun	1	6:09 AM (0.38) L
Mon	2 ○	6:36 AM (0.43) L
Tue	3	6:39 AM (0.51) L
Wed	4	6:28 AM (0.58) L
Thu	5	6:05 AM (0.62) L
Fri	6	5:34 AM (0.63) L
Sat	7	5:37 AM (0.61) L
Sun	8	5:37 AM (0.60) L
Mon	9	5:06 AM (0.58) L
Tue	10	4:58 AM (0.56) L
Wed	11	4:40 AM (0.54) L
Thu	12	4:18 AM (0.52) L
Fri	13	4:31 AM (0.50) L
Sat	14	4:48 AM (0.48) L
Sun	15	5:05 AM (0.48) L
Mon	16	5:16 AM (0.49) L
Tue	17 ●	5:24 AM (0.52) L
Wed	18	5:33 AM (0.55) L
Thu	19	5:42 AM (0.59) L
Fri	20	5:39 AM (0.63) L
Sat	21	5:21 AM (0.66) L
Sun	22	5:11 AM (0.66) L
Mon	23	4:20 AM (0.63) L
Tue	24	2:07 AM (0.56) L
Wed	25	2:40 AM (0.49) L
Thu	26	3:15 AM (0.44) L
Fri	27	3:52 AM (0.43) L
Sat	28	4:28 AM (0.44) L

Tide 2	Tide 3	Tide 4
9:16 PM (1.20) **H**		
9:55 PM (1.14) **H**		
1:04 PM (0.74) **H**	2:36 PM (0.73) L	10:23 PM (1.06) **H**
1:11 PM (0.79) **H**	3:30 PM (0.75) L	10:26 PM (0.97) **H**
1:15 PM (0.84) **H**	4:26 PM (0.78) L	10:20 PM (0.90) **H**
1:30 PM (0.89) **H**	5:34 PM (0.81) L	8:20 PM (0.85) **H**
1:54 PM (0.94) **H**	7:01 PM (0.84) L	8:15 PM (0.84) L
2:24 PM (0.98) **H**		
3:02 PM (1.01) **H**		
3:53 PM (1.03) **H**		
4:55 PM (1.06) **H**		
6:04 PM (1.08) **H**		
7:00 PM (1.12) **H**		
7:44 PM (1.14) **H**		
8:21 PM (1.16) **H**		
8:57 PM (1.15) **H**		
12:00 PM (0.78) **H**	2:13 PM (0.75) L	9:30 PM (1.12) **H**
12:01 PM (0.81) **H**	3:04 PM (0.74) L	10:01 PM (1.07) **H**
12:18 PM (0.86) **H**	3:58 PM (0.75) L	10:28 PM (0.99) **H**
12:41 PM (0.92) **H**	5:00 PM (0.75) L	10:48 PM (0.89) **H**
1:04 PM (0.97) **H**	6:22 PM (0.76) L	11:00 PM (0.79) **H**
1:30 PM (1.02) **H**		
2:09 PM (1.07) **H**		
3:01 PM (1.10) **H**		
4:00 PM (1.12) **H**		
5:13 PM (1.14) **H**		
6:51 PM (1.16) **H**		
7:49 PM (1.17) **H**		

Fremantle

POPULAR TIDE ADJUSTMENTS

Cervantes	-2min
Hillarys	-15min
Lancelin	0
Rottnest Island	-10min
Swan River Causeway	+1hr
Two Rocks Marina	-10min
Warnbro Sound	-10min
Bunbury	- 15min
Busselton	- 22min
Canning Bridge	+ 1hr 20min
Mandurah	- 2min
Peel Inlet	+ 3hr
Rockingham	+ 6min
Warnbro Sound	- 12min
Geraldton	- 30min
Kalbarri	- 30min

Day	Date		Tide 1
Sun	1		4:59 AM (0.48) L
Mon	2		5:13 AM (0.53) L
Tue	3	○	5:01 AM (0.59) L
Wed	4		5:03 AM (0.65) L
Thu	5		4:50 AM (0.69) L
Fri	6		4:17 AM (0.69) L
Sat	7		4:24 AM (0.67) L
Sun	8		4:25 AM (0.66) L
Mon	9		3:55 AM (0.64) L
Tue	10		3:55 AM (0.62) L
Wed	11		2:44 AM (0.61) L
Thu	12		2:58 AM (0.59) L
Fri	13		3:17 AM (0.57) L
Sat	14		3:37 AM (0.56) L
Sun	15		3:51 AM (0.57) L
Mon	16		4:00 AM (0.58) L
Tue	17		4:07 AM (0.60) L
Wed	18		4:16 AM (0.64) L
Thu	19	●	4:23 AM (0.68) L
Fri	20		4:11 AM (0.72) L
Sat	21		3:52 AM (0.74) L
Sun	22		12:59 AM (0.78) **H**
Mon	23		11:36 AM (1.18) **H**
Tue	24		12:40 AM (0.58) L
Wed	25		1:22 AM (0.53) L
Thu	26		2:02 AM (0.50) L
Fri	27		2:40 AM (0.51) L
Sat	28		3:15 AM (0.55) L
Sun	29		3:40 AM (0.60) L
Mon	30		3:44 AM (0.66) L
Tue	31		3:35 AM (0.71) L

Tide 2	Tide 3	Tide 4
8:35 PM (1.15) **H**		
11:39 AM (0.80) **H**	1:21 PM (0.79) L	9:15 PM (1.11) **H**
11:36 AM (0.83) **H**	2:28 PM (0.77) L	9:47 PM (1.05) **H**
11:45 AM (0.88) **H**	3:31 PM (0.76) L	10:10 PM (0.97) **H**
11:53 AM (0.93) **H**	4:35 PM (0.76) L	10:13 PM (0.89) **H**
12:00 PM (0.98) **H**	5:25 PM (0.77) L	10:15 PM (0.82) **H**
11:30 AM (1.03) **H**	6:13 PM (0.77) L	7:42 PM (0.79) **H**
11:35 AM (1.07) **H**		
12:00 PM (1.09) **H**		
12:31 PM (1.09) **H**		
1:08 PM (1.08) **H**		
3:36 PM (1.06) **H**		
5:00 PM (1.07) **H**		
6:32 PM (1.10) **H**		
7:27 PM (1.12) **H**		
11:34 AM (0.85) **H**	12:43 PM (0.85) L	8:09 PM (1.12) **H**
10:47 AM (0.87) **H**	1:53 PM (0.81) L	8:50 PM (1.10) **H**
10:45 AM (0.91) **H**	2:56 PM (0.78) L	9:32 PM (1.05) **H**
10:58 AM (0.97) **H**	4:04 PM (0.75) L	10:23 PM (0.97) **H**
11:14 AM (1.04) **H**	5:10 PM (0.72) L	11:54 PM (0.87) **H**
11:19 AM (1.10) **H**	6:24 PM (0.70) L	
3:39 AM (0.73) L	11:17 AM (1.15) **H**	11:55 PM (0.66) L
12:01 PM (1.19) **H**		
12:33 PM (1.16) **H**	1:31 PM (1.16) L	2:21 PM (1.16) L
3:26 PM (1.14) **H**		
4:39 PM (1.12) **H**		
6:53 PM (1.10) **H**		
7:46 PM (1.09) **H**		
10:23 AM (0.90) **H**	2:18 PM (0.86) L	8:30 PM (1.05) **H**
10:17 AM (0.95) **H**	3:17 PM (0.82) L	9:13 PM (1.00) **H**

Fremantle

POPULAR TIDE ADJUSTMENTS

Cervantes	-2min
Hillarys	-15min
Lancelin	0
Rottnest Island	-10min
Swan River Causeway	+1hr
Two Rocks Marina	-10min
Warnbro Sound	-10min
Bunbury	- 15min
Busselton	- 22min
Canning Bridge	+ 1hr 20min
Mandurah	- 2min
Peel Inlet	+ 3hr
Rockingham	+ 6min
Warnbro Sound	- 12min
Geraldton	- 30min
Kalbarri	- 30min

Day	Date	Tide 5
Sun	5	11:48 PM (0.73) L
Sun	6	10:50 PM (0.71) **H**

Day	Date	Tide 1
Wed	1	3:36 AM (0.75) L
Thu	2 ○	2:55 AM (0.77) L
Fri	3	2:51 AM (0.76) L
Sat	4	3:04 AM (0.76) L
Sun	5*	3:03 AM (0.75) L
Mon	6*	1:09 AM (0.74) **H**
Tue	7	12:26 AM (0.70) L
Wed	8	1:01 AM (0.68) L
Thu	9	1:31 AM (0.66) L
Fri	10	1:59 AM (0.65) L
Sat	11	2:21 AM (0.65) L
Sun	12	2:36 AM (0.66) L
Mon	13	2:42 AM (0.68) L
Tue	14	2:45 AM (0.71) L
Wed	15	2:48 AM (0.75) L
Thu	16	2:47 AM (0.79) L
Fri	17 ●	2:33 AM (0.82) L
Sat	18	2:20 AM (0.83) L
Sun	19	12:37 AM (0.82) **H**
Mon	20	10:37 AM (1.31) **H**
Tue	21	11:05 AM (1.30) **H**
Wed	22	11:34 AM (1.27) **H**
Thu	23	12:45 AM (0.56) L
Fri	24	1:28 AM (0.59) L
Sat	25	2:03 AM (0.65) L
Sun	26	2:30 AM (0.71) L
Mon	27	2:30 AM (0.78) L
Tue	28	2:04 AM (0.83) L
Wed	29	1:41 AM (0.85) L
Thu	30	1:05 AM (0.85) L

* Additional Tide 5 - See Additional Tide 5

Tide 2	Tide 3	Tide 4
10:24 AM (1.00) **H**	4:03 PM (0.78) L	9:56 PM (0.95) **H**
10:24 AM (1.06) **H**	4:45 PM (0.76) L	10:47 PM (0.88) **H**
10:14 AM (1.11) **H**	5:24 PM (0.75) L	11:38 PM (0.83) **H**
10:15 AM (1.15) **H**	7:55 PM (0.73) L	10:29 PM (0.77) **H**
10:30 AM (1.18) **H**	8:49 PM (0.72) L	10:36 PM (0.74) **H**
2:35 AM (0.73) L	10:55 AM (1.20) **H**	9:39 PM (0.70) L
1:59 AM (0.71) **H**	2:36 AM (0.71) L	11:23 AM (1.19) **H**
11:54 AM (1.18) **H**		
12:28 PM (1.15) **H**		
1:07 PM (1.12) **H**		
3:45 PM (1.10) **H**		
5:15 PM (1.09) **H**		
10:54 AM (0.95) **H**	12:04 PM (0.95) L	6:49 PM (1.08) **H**
9:27 AM (0.97) **H**	1:31 PM (0.90) L	7:53 PM (1.06) **H**
9:16 AM (1.03) **H**	2:55 PM (0.83) L	9:00 PM (1.01) **H**
9:24 AM (1.10) **H**	3:59 PM (0.76) L	10:23 PM (0.95) **H**
9:36 AM (1.17) **H**	5:00 PM (0.70) L	11:31 PM (0.89) **H**
9:52 AM (1.24) **H**	6:40 PM (0.65) L	
1:57 AM (0.81) L	10:12 AM (1.29) **H**	8:09 PM (0.60) L
9:15 PM (0.58) L		
11:56 PM (0.56) L		
12:04 PM (1.21) **H**		
12:35 PM (1.14) **H**	1:28 PM (1.14) L	2:56 PM (1.15) **H**
3:56 PM (1.09) **H**		
10:33 AM (1.00) **H**	11:56 AM (0.99) L	6:14 PM (1.03) **H**
9:07 AM (1.01) **H**	2:24 PM (0.93) L	7:30 PM (0.99) **H**
8:55 AM (1.06) **H**	3:04 PM (0.88) L	8:44 PM (0.95) **H**
8:53 AM (1.12) **H**	3:46 PM (0.83) L	9:53 PM (0.91) **H**
8:46 AM (1.18) **H**	4:32 PM (0.78) L	10:45 PM (0.88) **H**

POPULAR TIDE ADJUSTMENTS

Cervantes	-2min
Hillarys	-15min
Lancelin	0
Rottnest Island	-10min
Swan River Causeway	+1hr
Two Rocks Marina	-10min
Warnbro Sound	-10min
Bunbury	- 15min
Busselton	- 22min
Canning Bridge	+ 1hr 20min
Mandurah	- 2min
Peel Inlet	+ 3hr
Rockingham	+ 6min
Warnbro Sound	- 12min
Geraldton	- 30min
Kalbarri	- 30min

Fremantle

Day	Date		Tide 1
Fri	1		1:22 AM (0.84) L
Sat	2	○	1:40 AM (0.83) L
Sun	3		12:21 AM (0.83) **H**
Mon	4		9:56 AM (1.29) **H**
Tue	5		10:25 AM (1.29) **H**
Wed	6		10:56 AM (1.27) **H**
Thu	7		11:29 AM (1.25) **H**
Fri	8		12:31 AM (0.73) L
Sat	9		1:00 AM (0.74) L
Sun	10		1:14 AM (0.75) L
Mon	11		12:51 AM (0.78) L
Tue	12		12:55 AM (0.80) L
Wed	13		1:03 AM (0.84) L
Thu	14		1:06 AM (0.88) L
Fri	15		12:51 AM (0.90) L
Sat	16		12:02 AM (0.90) L
Sun	17	●	9:13 AM (1.40) **H**
Mon	18		9:45 AM (1.41) **H**
Tue	19		10:22 AM (1.39) **H**
Wed	20		11:00 AM (1.35) **H**
Thu	21		11:28 AM (1.28) **H**
Fri	22		12:08 AM (0.65) L
Sat	23		12:52 AM (0.72) L
Sun	24		1:24 AM (0.80) L
Mon	25		1:08 AM (0.87) L
Tue	26		7:36 AM (1.13) **H**
Wed	27		7:35 AM (1.19) **H**
Thu	28		7:37 AM (1.24) **H**
Fri	29		7:51 AM (1.29) **H**
Sat	30		8:11 AM (1.32) **H**
Sun	31	○	8:35 AM (1.34) **H**

Tide 2	Tide 3	Tide 4
8:54 AM (1.23) **H**	5:36 PM (0.74) L	11:32 PM (0.85) **H**
9:10 AM (1.26) **H**	6:50 PM (0.71) L	
1:34 AM (0.83) L	9:30 AM (1.29) **H**	7:35 PM (0.70) L
8:17 PM (0.69) L		
9:00 PM (0.70) L		
9:45 PM (0.71) L		
10:36 PM (0.73) L	11:30 PM (0.73) L	
12:01 PM (1.22) **H**		
12:38 PM (1.18) **H**		
1:20 PM (1.13) **H**		
3:42 PM (1.07) **H**		
8:02 AM (1.05) **H**	12:51 PM (0.98) L	5:45 PM (1.01) **H**
7:50 AM (1.12) **H**	2:38 PM (0.89) L	8:06 PM (0.96) **H**
7:59 AM (1.20) **H**	3:43 PM (0.79) L	10:00 PM (0.93) **H**
8:17 AM (1.28) **H**	4:51 PM (0.70) L	11:25 PM (0.90) **H**
8:43 AM (1.35) **H**	6:11 PM (0.62) L	
7:11 PM (0.57) L		
8:06 PM (0.55) L		
9:07 PM (0.57) L		
11:09 PM (0.60) L		
11:43 AM (1.20) **H**	12:42 PM (1.20) L	1:38 PM (1.20) L
12:00 PM (1.12) **H**	1:31 PM (1.11) L	2:19 PM (1.12) **H**
9:43 AM (1.06) **H**	11:07 AM (1.05) L	12:10 PM (1.06) **H**
7:56 AM (1.07) **H**	9:34 PM (0.90) L	
6:54 PM (0.89) L	8:34 PM (0.89) L	9:46 PM (0.89) L
5:14 PM (0.83) L		
5:34 PM (0.78) L		
5:52 PM (0.74) L		
6:13 PM (0.71) L		
6:41 PM (0.69) L		

Fremantle

POPULAR TIDE ADJUSTMENTS

Cervantes	-2min
Hillarys	-15min
Lancelin	0
Rottnest Island	-10min
Swan River Causeway	+1hr
Two Rocks Marina	-10min
Warnbro Sound	-10min
Bunbury	- 15min
Busselton	- 22min
Canning Bridge	+ 1hr 20min
Mandurah	- 2min
Peel Inlet	+ 3hr
Rockingham	+ 6min
Warnbro Sound	- 12min
Geraldton	- 30min
Kalbarri	- 30min

Day	Date	Tide 1
Mon	1	9:04 AM (1.34) **H**
Tue	2	9:35 AM (1.34) **H**
Wed	3	10:09 AM (1.32) **H**
Thu	4	10:42 AM (1.30) **H**
Fri	5	11:15 AM (1.26) **H**
Sat	6	11:46 AM (1.22) **H**
Sun	7	12:17 PM (1.17) **H**
Mon	8	12:47 PM (1.11) **H**
Tue	9	6:51 AM (1.07) **H**
Wed	10	6:33 AM (1.13) **H**
Thu	11	6:40 AM (1.22) **H**
Fri	12	7:05 AM (1.30) **H**
Sat	13	7:38 AM (1.37) **H**
Sun	14	8:16 AM (1.42) **H**
Mon	15 ●	9:00 AM (1.44) **H**
Tue	16	9:47 AM (1.43) **H**
Wed	17	10:42 AM (1.38) **H**
Thu	18	11:43 AM (1.31) **H**
Fri	19	12:31 PM (1.22) **H**
Sat	20	11:17 AM (1.13) **H**
Sun	21	9:19 AM (1.06) **H**
Mon	22	8:37 AM (1.05) **H**
Tue	23	6:20 AM (1.11) **H**
Wed	24	6:25 AM (1.17) **H**
Thu	25	6:32 AM (1.22) **H**
Fri	26	6:52 AM (1.26) **H**
Sat	27	7:18 AM (1.29) **H**
Sun	28	7:47 AM (1.31) **H**
Mon	29	8:20 AM (1.32) **H**
Tue	30 ○	8:55 AM (1.32) **H**

Tide 2		Tide 3		Tide 4	
7:15 PM	(0.68) L				
7:50 PM	(0.68) L				
8:27 PM	(0.70) L				
9:02 PM	(0.72) L				
9:37 PM	(0.75) L				
10:08 PM	(0.78) L				
10:32 PM	(0.81) L				
10:42 PM	(0.85) L				
12:00 PM	(1.02) L	1:08 PM	(1.02) L	9:30 PM	(0.88) L
8:55 PM	(0.89) L				
4:16 PM	(0.80) L				
4:51 PM	(0.70) L				
5:35 PM	(0.60) L				
6:22 PM	(0.54) L				
7:10 PM	(0.52) L				
7:58 PM	(0.54) L				
8:47 PM	(0.59) L				
9:38 PM	(0.67) L				
10:07 PM	(0.76) L				
9:54 PM	(0.83) L				
10:02 AM	(1.06) L	11:17 AM	(1.06) L	7:31 PM	(0.86) L
7:29 PM	(0.84) L				
7:04 PM	(0.82) L				
6:17 PM	(0.79) L				
5:25 PM	(0.75) L				
5:27 PM	(0.72) L				
5:41 PM	(0.69) L				
5:59 PM	(0.67) L				
6:24 PM	(0.66) L				
6:53 PM	(0.66) L				

POPULAR TIDE ADJUSTMENTS

Cervantes	-2min
Hillarys	-15min
Lancelin	0
Rottnest Island	-10min
Swan River Causeway	+1hr
Two Rocks Marina	-10min
Warnbro Sound	-10min
Bunbury	- 15min
Busselton	- 22min
Canning Bridge	+ 1hr 20min
Mandurah	- 2min
Peel Inlet	+ 3hr
Rockingham	+ 6min
Warnbro Sound	- 12min
Geraldton	- 30min
Kalbarri	- 30min

Fremantle

Day	Date	Tide 1
Wed	1	9:30 AM (1.31) **H**
Thu	2	10:05 AM (1.29) **H**
Fri	3	10:38 AM (1.26) **H**
Sat	4	11:07 AM (1.21) **H**
Sun	5	11:34 AM (1.15) **H**
Mon	6	11:58 AM (1.08) **H**
Tue	7	3:55 AM (1.01) **H**
Wed	8	4:25 AM (1.08) **H**
Thu	9	5:01 AM (1.16) **H**
Fri	10	5:43 AM (1.23) **H**
Sat	11	6:30 AM (1.30) **H**
Sun	12	7:19 AM (1.36) **H**
Mon	13	8:12 AM (1.39) **H**
Tue	14 ●	9:04 AM (1.38) **H**
Wed	15	9:57 AM (1.35) **H**
Thu	16	10:48 AM (1.28) **H**
Fri	17	11:32 AM (1.19) **H**
Sat	18	2:46 AM (0.86) **H**
Sun	19	2:57 AM (0.91) **H**
Mon	20	2:46 AM (0.98) **H**
Tue	21	3:14 AM (1.03) **H**
Wed	22	3:54 AM (1.08) **H**
Thu	23	4:40 AM (1.12) **H**
Fri	24	5:30 AM (1.15) **H**
Sat	25	6:18 AM (1.18) **H**
Sun	26	7:01 AM (1.21) **H**
Mon	27	7:42 AM (1.22) **H**
Tue	28	8:20 AM (1.24) **H**
Wed	29	8:56 AM (1.24) **H**
Thu	30 ○	12:50 AM (0.81) **H**
Fri	31	12:28 AM (0.82) **H**

Tide 2	Tide 3	Tide 4
7:22 PM (0.67) L		
7:46 PM (0.69) L		
7:57 PM (0.72) L		
7:45 PM (0.75) L		
7:41 PM (0.78) L		
7:37 PM (0.80) L		
7:42 AM (0.99) L	9:30 AM (1.00) H	7:30 PM (0.82) L
6:58 PM (0.82) L		
3:51 PM (0.76) L		
4:13 PM (0.66) L		
4:48 PM (0.58) L		
5:30 PM (0.52) L		
6:14 PM (0.50) L		
6:57 PM (0.51) L		
7:37 PM (0.56) L		
8:10 PM (0.64) L		
8:18 PM (0.73) L		
3:34 AM (0.86) L	11:18 AM (1.09) H	7:20 PM (0.80) L
4:39 AM (0.91) L	10:47 AM (1.00) H	6:17 PM (0.80) L
6:06 AM (0.95) L	8:29 AM (0.97) H	6:16 PM (0.77) L
6:08 PM (0.75) L		
5:31 PM (0.72) L		
5:26 PM (0.69) L		
4:50 PM (0.67) L		
4:56 PM (0.65) L		
5:11 PM (0.63) L		
5:30 PM (0.62) L		
5:53 PM (0.62) L		
6:13 PM (0.63) L		
1:39 AM (0.81) L	9:30 AM (1.22) H	6:19 PM (0.65) L
2:34 AM (0.81) L	10:01 AM (1.19) H	6:21 PM (0.68) L

POPULAR TIDE ADJUSTMENTS

Cervantes	-2min
Hillarys	-15min
Lancelin	0
Rottnest Island	-10min
Swan River Causeway	+1hr
Two Rocks Marina	-10min
Warnbro Sound	-10min
Bunbury	- 15min
Busselton	- 22min
Canning Bridge	+ 1hr 20min
Mandurah	- 2min
Peel Inlet	+ 3hr
Rockingham	+ 6min
Warnbro Sound	- 12min
Geraldton	- 30min
Kalbarri	- 30min

Day	Date	Tide 5
Mon	17	11:45 PM (1.00) **H**
Tue	18	4:48 PM (0.69) L

Fremantle

Day	Date	Tide 1
Sat	1	12:37 AM (0.85) **H**
Sun	2	12:58 AM (0.88) **H**
Mon	3	1:24 AM (0.93) **H**
Tue	4	1:55 AM (0.98) **H**
Wed	5	2:30 AM (1.03) **H**
Thu	6	3:12 AM (1.08) **H**
Fri	7	4:01 AM (1.13) **H**
Sat	8	5:01 AM (1.18) **H**
Sun	9	6:12 AM (1.22) **H**
Mon	10	7:21 AM (1.26) **H**
Tue	11	8:18 AM (1.27) **H**
Wed	12	9:09 AM (1.25) **H**
Thu	13 ●	12:19 AM (0.78) **H**
Fri	14	12:16 AM (0.80) **H**
Sat	15	12:29 AM (0.85) **H**
Sun	16	12:41 AM (0.90) **H**
Mon	17*	12:56 AM (0.95) **H**
Tue	18*	12:29 AM (0.99) L
Wed	19	12:07 AM (1.03) **H**
Thu	20	12:43 AM (1.05) **H**
Fri	21	1:32 AM (1.04) **H**
Sat	22	4:18 AM (1.05) **H**
Sun	23	5:40 AM (1.06) **H**
Mon	24	6:57 AM (1.09) **H**
Tue	25	7:42 AM (1.11) **H**
Wed	26	8:18 AM (1.12) **H**
Thu	27	1:24 AM (0.77) L
Fri	28 ○	2:15 AM (0.75) L
Sat	29	3:03 AM (0.73) L
Sun	30	3:54 AM (0.72) L
Mon	31	4:51 AM (0.71) L

* Additional Tide 5 - See Additional Tide 5

AUGUST 2026

Tide 2		Tide 3		Tide 4	
3:21 AM	(0.81) L	10:30 AM	(1.14) **H**	6:24 PM	(0.71) L
4:11 AM	(0.83) L	10:56 AM	(1.07) **H**	6:23 PM	(0.73) L
5:08 AM	(0.85) L	11:18 AM	(0.99) **H**	6:15 PM	(0.75) L
6:29 AM	(0.87) L	11:34 AM	(0.91) **H**	6:09 PM	(0.76) L
5:20 PM	(0.74) L				
2:46 PM	(0.69) L	3:51 PM	(0.69) L	4:43 PM	(0.69) L
3:13 PM	(0.60) L				
3:47 PM	(0.53) L				
4:26 PM	(0.49) L				
5:06 PM	(0.48) L				
5:45 PM	(0.50) L				
6:19 PM	(0.55) L				
1:25 AM	(0.77) L	9:57 AM	(1.19) **H**	6:29 PM	(0.62) L
2:31 AM	(0.77) L	10:41 AM	(1.11) **H**	6:08 PM	(0.70) L
3:28 AM	(0.78) L	11:15 AM	(1.01) **H**	5:50 PM	(0.75) L
4:28 AM	(0.80) L	10:39 AM	(0.91) **H**	4:59 PM	(0.74) L
5:41 AM	(0.82) L	10:27 AM	(0.84) **H**	5:00 PM	(0.72) L
1:16 AM	(1.00) **H**	6:51 AM	(0.84) L	7:57 AM	(0.84) L
4:22 PM	(0.66) L				
4:28 PM	(0.63) L				
2:17 AM	(1.04) L	3:15 AM	(1.05) **H**	3:30 PM	(0.62) L
3:45 PM	(0.60) L				
4:02 PM	(0.59) L				
4:20 PM	(0.59) L				
4:34 PM	(0.59) L				
4:45 PM	(0.60) L	11:18 PM	(0.79) **H**		
8:52 AM	(1.12) **H**	4:52 PM	(0.62) L	11:08 PM	(0.81) **H**
9:25 AM	(1.09) **H**	5:00 PM	(0.65) L	11:15 PM	(0.84) **H**
9:57 AM	(1.04) **H**	5:05 PM	(0.68) L	11:29 PM	(0.88) **H**
10:26 AM	(0.97) **H**	4:57 PM	(0.70) L	11:39 PM	(0.93) **H**
10:48 AM	(0.88) **H**	4:45 PM	(0.71) L	11:27 PM	(0.98) **H**

Fremantle

POPULAR TIDE ADJUSTMENTS

Cervantes	-2min
Hillarys	-15min
Lancelin	0
Rottnest Island	-10min
Swan River Causeway	+1hr
Two Rocks Marina	-10min
Warnbro Sound	-10min
Bunbury	- 15min
Busselton	- 22min
Canning Bridge	+ 1hr 20min
Mandurah	- 2min
Peel Inlet	+ 3hr
Rockingham	+ 6min
Warnbro Sound	- 12min
Geraldton	- 30min
Kalbarri	- 30min

Day	Date	Tide 1
Tue	1	5:57 AM (0.72) L
Wed	2*	10:00 AM (0.69) L
Thu	3	12:05 AM (1.06) **H**
Fri	4	12:37 AM (1.07) **H**
Sat	5	3:21 AM (1.07) **H**
Sun	6	4:31 AM (1.08) **H**
Mon	7	6:15 AM (1.10) **H**
Tue	8	7:31 AM (1.11) **H**
Wed	9	8:24 AM (1.10) **H**
Thu	10	1:39 AM (0.74) L
Fri	11 ●	3:16 AM (0.71) L
Sat	12	4:14 AM (0.69) L
Sun	13	4:58 AM (0.68) L
Mon	14	5:37 AM (0.68) L
Tue	15	12:05 PM (0.67) L
Wed	16	12:45 PM (0.63) L
Thu	17	1:23 PM (0.59) L
Fri	18	1:56 PM (0.58) L
Sat	19	12:35 AM (1.01) **H**
Sun	20	1:21 AM (0.97) **H**
Mon	21	4:32 AM (0.96) **H**
Tue	22	6:32 AM (0.97) **H**
Wed	23	7:26 AM (0.99) **H**
Thu	24	1:00 AM (0.76) L
Fri	25	1:57 AM (0.72) L
Sat	26	2:54 AM (0.67) L
Sun	27 ○	3:54 AM (0.63) L
Mon	28	4:51 AM (0.60) L
Tue	29	5:53 AM (0.58) L
Wed	30	8:36 AM (0.55) L

Day	Date	Tide 5
Wed	2	3:47 PM (0.68) L

* Additional Tide 5 - See Additional Tide 5

Tide 2		Tide 3		Tide 4	
11:04 AM	(0.79) **H**	4:37 PM	(0.71) L	11:41 PM	(1.02) **H**
11:11 AM	(0.70) **H**	12:58 PM	(0.68) L	2:14 PM	(0.69) **H**
1:29 PM	(0.60) L				
2:03 PM	(0.53) L				
2:39 PM	(0.48) L				
3:15 PM	(0.46) L				
3:50 PM	(0.47) L				
4:20 PM	(0.51) L				
4:30 PM	(0.56) L	10:46 PM	(0.78) **H**		
9:12 AM	(1.06) **H**	4:27 PM	(0.62) L	10:49 PM	(0.82) **H**
10:00 AM	(0.99) **H**	4:32 PM	(0.68) L	11:00 PM	(0.87) **H**
10:49 AM	(0.91) **H**	4:09 PM	(0.71) L	11:03 PM	(0.92) **H**
11:37 AM	(0.82) **H**	3:32 PM	(0.70) L	10:36 PM	(0.97) **H**
12:21 PM	(0.74) **H**	3:41 PM	(0.68) L	10:37 PM	(1.01) **H**
1:03 PM	(0.68) **H**	3:20 PM	(0.65) L	10:58 PM	(1.04) **H**
1:47 PM	(0.63) L	3:05 PM	(0.62) L	11:26 PM	(1.05) **H**
2:42 PM	(0.60) **H**	3:10 PM	(0.60) L	11:59 PM	(1.03) **H**
2:23 PM	(0.57) L				
2:46 PM	(0.56) L				
3:05 PM	(0.56) L				
3:18 PM	(0.57) L				
3:25 PM	(0.59) L	10:02 PM	(0.79) **H**		
8:08 AM	(0.99) **H**	3:31 PM	(0.61) L	9:42 PM	(0.82) **H**
8:48 AM	(0.97) **H**	3:37 PM	(0.64) L	9:42 PM	(0.87) **H**
9:34 AM	(0.93) **H**	3:33 PM	(0.67) L	9:46 PM	(0.92) **H**
10:40 AM	(0.86) **H**	3:20 PM	(0.69) L	9:56 PM	(0.98) **H**
11:49 AM	(0.79) **H**	3:15 PM	(0.70) L	10:11 PM	(1.03) **H**
12:50 PM	(0.71) **H**	3:00 PM	(0.69) L	10:31 PM	(1.07) **H**
10:58 PM	(1.09) **H**				

POPULAR TIDE ADJUSTMENTS

Cervantes	-2min
Hillarys	-15min
Lancelin	0
Rottnest Island	-10min
Swan River Causeway	+1hr
Two Rocks Marina	-10min
Warnbro Sound	-10min
Bunbury	- 15min
Busselton	- 22min
Canning Bridge	+ 1hr 20min
Mandurah	- 2min
Peel Inlet	+ 3hr
Rockingham	+ 6min
Warnbro Sound	- 12min
Geraldton	- 30min
Kalbarri	- 30min

Fremantle

Day	Date	Tide 1
Thu	1	9:46 AM (0.52) L
Fri	2	12:47 PM (0.47) L
Sat	3	12:00 AM (1.06) **H**
Sun	4	12:39 AM (1.01) **H**
Mon	5	4:03 AM (0.98) **H**
Tue	6	6:28 AM (0.96) **H**
Wed	7	12:35 AM (0.78) L
Thu	8	2:09 AM (0.72) L
Fri	9	3:07 AM (0.66) L
Sat	10	3:55 AM (0.62) L
Sun	11 ●	4:41 AM (0.59) L
Mon	12	5:29 AM (0.57) L
Tue	13	7:25 AM (0.56) L
Wed	14	8:21 AM (0.55) L
Thu	15	9:07 AM (0.55) L
Fri	16	9:55 AM (0.56) L
Sat	17	1:03 PM (0.56) L
Sun	18	1:32 PM (0.56) L
Mon	19	12:34 AM (0.95) **H**
Tue	20	1:18 AM (0.91) **H**
Wed	21	4:42 AM (0.88) **H**
Thu	22	12:36 AM (0.79) L
Fri	23	1:50 AM (0.72) L
Sat	24	2:55 AM (0.65) L
Sun	25	3:48 AM (0.58) L
Mon	26 ○	4:43 AM (0.51) L
Tue	27	5:50 AM (0.46) L
Wed	28	7:21 AM (0.42) L
Thu	29	8:26 AM (0.41) L
Fri	30	9:29 AM (0.42) L
Sat	31	12:05 PM (0.43) L

Tide 2	Tide 3	Tide 4
10:55 AM (0.53) **H**	12:00 PM (0.52) L	11:27 PM (1.09) **H**
1:29 PM (0.45) L		
1:38 AM (1.01) L	2:53 AM (1.02) **H**	2:06 PM (0.45) L
2:40 PM (0.48) L		
3:05 PM (0.53) L	10:30 PM (0.79) **H**	
7:35 AM (0.95) **H**	3:09 PM (0.60) L	9:21 PM (0.81) **H**
8:33 AM (0.91) **H**	3:00 PM (0.65) L	9:20 PM (0.86) **H**
9:33 AM (0.86) **H**	2:59 PM (0.69) L	9:16 PM (0.92) **H**
10:29 AM (0.81) **H**	2:05 PM (0.70) L	9:12 PM (0.98) **H**
11:17 AM (0.75) **H**	2:11 PM (0.69) L	9:20 PM (1.03) **H**
12:02 PM (0.70) **H**	2:22 PM (0.67) L	9:35 PM (1.06) **H**
12:46 PM (0.65) **H**	1:58 PM (0.65) L	9:56 PM (1.08) **H**
10:21 PM (1.08) **H**		
10:52 AM (0.57) **H**	11:45 AM (0.57) L	10:51 PM (1.06) **H**
11:04 AM (0.57) **H**	12:28 PM (0.56) L	11:24 PM (1.03) **H**
11:58 PM (1.00) **H**		
1:54 PM (0.57) L		
2:06 PM (0.58) L	10:49 PM (0.84) **H**	11:16 PM (0.84) L
2:05 PM (0.60) L	8:52 PM (0.83) **H**	
6:48 AM (0.86) **H**	2:01 PM (0.63) L	8:21 PM (0.87) **H**
8:00 AM (0.85) **H**	2:01 PM (0.66) L	8:20 PM (0.92) **H**
9:15 AM (0.82) **H**	1:58 PM (0.69) L	8:30 PM (0.99) **H**
10:26 AM (0.78) **H**	1:53 PM (0.71) L	8:46 PM (1.06) **H**
11:27 AM (0.74) **H**	1:44 PM (0.71) L	9:07 PM (1.11) **H**
12:38 PM (0.69) **H**	1:08 PM (0.69) L	9:31 PM (1.15) **H**
10:00 PM (1.16) **H**		
10:30 PM (1.15) **H**		
11:02 PM (1.10) **H**		
11:33 PM (1.04) **H**		

POPULAR TIDE ADJUSTMENTS

Cervantes	-2min
Hillarys	-15min
Lancelin	0
Rottnest Island	-10min
Swan River Causeway	+1hr
Two Rocks Marina	-10min
Warnbro Sound	-10min
Bunbury	- 15min
Busselton	- 22min
Canning Bridge	+ 1hr 20min
Mandurah	- 2min
Peel Inlet	+ 3hr
Rockingham	+ 6min
Warnbro Sound	- 12min
Geraldton	- 30min
Kalbarri	- 30min

Day	Date	Tide 5
Tue	3	9:27 PM (0.84) **H**

Fremantle

Day	Date	Tide 1
Sun	1	12:03 AM (0.46) **H**
Mon	2	12:03 AM (0.96) L
Tue	3*	12:30 AM (0.88) **H**
Wed	4	2:20 AM (0.79) L
Thu	5	2:53 AM (0.72) L
Fri	6	3:24 AM (0.65) L
Sat	7	4:00 AM (0.59) L
Sun	8	4:49 AM (0.54) L
Mon	9 ●	5:44 AM (0.50) L
Tue	10	6:26 AM (0.48) L
Wed	11	7:06 AM (0.47) L
Thu	12	7:45 AM (0.48) L
Fri	13	8:24 AM (0.50) L
Sat	14	9:05 AM (0.52) L
Sun	15	9:46 AM (0.55) L
Mon	16	12:09 AM (0.58) **H**
Tue	17	12:00 AM (0.96) L
Wed	18	12:28 AM (0.90) **H**
Thu	19	11:58 AM (0.66) L
Fri	20	12:06 PM (0.69) L
Sat	21	3:18 AM (0.66) L
Sun	22	3:50 AM (0.57) L
Mon	23	4:39 AM (0.47) L
Tue	24	5:34 AM (0.39) L
Wed	25 ○	6:30 AM (0.34) L
Thu	26	7:22 AM (0.33) L
Fri	27	8:12 AM (0.35) L
Sat	28	9:03 AM (0.40) L
Sun	29	9:59 AM (0.47) L
Mon	30	12:05 PM (0.55) L

* Additional Tide 5 - See Additional Tide 5

NOVEMBER 2026

Tide 2		Tide 3		Tide 4	
1:25 AM	(0.96) L	2:25 AM	(0.96) L	1:30 PM	(0.51) L
1:49 AM	(0.88) L	3:27 AM	(0.89) **H**	1:58 PM	(0.58) L
4:56 AM	(0.82) **H**	1:56 PM	(0.65) L	8:04 PM	(0.87) **H**
7:50 AM	(0.78) **H**	1:15 PM	(0.69) L	8:03 PM	(0.93) **H**
9:20 AM	(0.75) **H**	12:28 PM	(0.71) L	8:00 PM	(1.00) **H**
10:17 AM	(0.72) **H**	12:12 PM	(0.70) L	8:04 PM	(1.05) **H**
11:08 AM	(0.70) **H**	12:31 PM	(0.69) **L**	8:20 PM	(1.10) **H**
8:39 PM	(1.12) **H**				
9:00 PM	(1.14) **H**				
9:26 PM	(1.13) **H**				
9:55 PM	(1.11) **H**				
10:26 PM	(1.08) **H**				
10:58 PM	(1.05) **H**				
11:30 PM	(1.01) **H**				
11:08 AM	(0.61) L				
11:38 AM	(0.63) L	8:42 PM	(0.87) **H**		
7:19 PM	(0.90) **H**				
7:15 PM	(0.97) **H**				
9:16 AM	(0.72) **H**	11:57 AM	(0.72) L	7:24 PM	(1.04) **H**
7:44 PM	(1.12) **H**				
8:10 PM	(1.18) **H**				
8:40 PM	(1.22) **H**				
9:13 PM	(1.24) **H**				
9:48 PM	(1.22) **H**				
10:24 PM	(1.17) **H**				
10:54 PM	(1.09) **H**				
11:13 PM	(1.00) **H**				
11:24 PM	(0.92) **H**				

POPULAR TIDE ADJUSTMENTS

Cervantes	-2min
Hillarys	-15min
Lancelin	0
Rottnest Island	-10min
Swan River Causeway	+1hr
Two Rocks Marina	-10min
Warnbro Sound	-10min
Bunbury	- 15min
Busselton	- 22min
Canning Bridge	+ 1hr 20min
Mandurah	- 2min
Peel Inlet	+ 3hr
Rockingham	+ 6min
Warnbro Sound	- 12min
Geraldton	- 30min
Kalbarri	- 30min

Fremantle

Day	Date	Tide 1
Tue	1	10:48 AM (0.63) L
Wed	2	8:11 AM (0.68) L
Thu	3	7:48 AM (0.67) L
Fri	4	5:30 AM (0.62) L
Sat	5	4:54 AM (0.56) L
Sun	6	5:17 AM (0.51) L
Mon	7	5:39 AM (0.47) L
Tue	8	5:58 AM (0.45) L
Wed	9 ●	6:18 AM (0.44) L
Thu	10	6:45 AM (0.44) L
Fri	11	7:15 AM (0.45) L
Sat	12	7:43 AM (0.48) L
Sun	13	8:04 AM (0.51) L
Mon	14	8:01 AM (0.55) L
Tue	15	7:58 AM (0.58) L
Wed	16	8:00 AM (0.61) L
Thu	17	7:59 AM (0.63) L
Fri	18	7:51 AM (0.65) L
Sat	19	6:32 AM (0.64) L
Sun	20	4:28 AM (0.57) L
Mon	21	4:43 AM (0.47) L
Tue	22	5:13 AM (0.38) L
Wed	23	5:50 AM (0.32) L
Thu	24 ○	6:31 AM (0.29) L
Fri	25	7:13 AM (0.31) L
Sat	26	7:52 AM (0.37) L
Sun	27	8:26 AM (0.45) L
Mon	28	8:44 AM (0.54) L
Tue	29	8:10 AM (0.62) L
Wed	30	6:52 AM (0.63) L
Thu	31	6:45 AM (0.61) L

Tide 2		Tide 3		Tide 4	
11:45 AM	(0.63) L	12:42 PM	(0.63) L	8:49 PM	(0.88) **H**
9:57 AM	(0.69) **H**	10:43 AM	(0.69) L	7:03 PM	(0.90) **H**
7:02 PM	(0.97) **H**				
7:05 PM	(1.04) **H**				
7:11 PM	(1.09) **H**				
7:28 PM	(1.13) **H**				
7:50 PM	(1.16) **H**				
8:15 PM	(1.17) **H**				
8:42 PM	(1.17) **H**				
9:12 PM	(1.15) **H**				
9:44 PM	(1.13) **H**				
10:15 PM	(1.10) **H**				
10:45 PM	(1.06) **H**				
11:11 PM	(1.01) **H**				
11:31 PM	(0.95) **H**				
9:42 PM	(0.89) **H**				
6:21 PM	(0.90) **H**				
6:05 PM	(0.97) **H**				
6:14 PM	(1.05) **H**				
6:40 PM	(1.13) **H**				
7:14 PM	(1.20) **H**				
7:52 PM	(1.25) **H**				
8:34 PM	(1.27) **H**				
9:18 PM	(1.26) **H**				
10:04 PM	(1.22) **H**				
10:46 PM	(1.14) **H**				
11:06 PM	(1.04) **H**				
10:51 PM	(0.94) **H**				
8:33 PM	(0.88) **H**				
5:45 PM	(0.89) **H**				
5:52 PM	(0.96) **H**				

Apogee moon phase on Friday 24th
Perigee moon phase on Wednesday 8th
● **New moon on Tuesday 21st**
First quarter moon on Thursday 30th
○ **Full moon on Tuesday 7th**
Last quarter moon phase on Tuesday 14th

Perth, WA: Rise: 05:30am Set: 06:20pm

(Note: These sun rise/set times are averages for the month)

DAY	MINOR BITE	MAJOR BITE	MINOR BITE	MAJOR BITE	SALT WATER RATING	FRESH WATER RATING
WED 1	10:42 AM	6:28 PM	1:24 AM	6:01 AM	5	6
THUR 2	11:48 AM	7:19 PM	2:05 AM	6:53 AM	4	5
FRI 3	12:57 PM	8:09 PM	2:40 AM	7:44 AM	3	5
SAT 4	2:07 PM	8:58 PM	3:10 AM	8:33 AM	6	6
SUN 5	3:17 PM	9:47 PM	3:38 AM	9:22 AM	5	7
MON 6	4:30 PM	10:36 PM	4:04 AM	10:11 AM	3	8
TUE 7	5:44 PM	11:27 PM	4:30 AM	11:01 AM	○ 5	7
WED 8	7:01 PM		4:59 AM	11:54 AM	7	6
THUR 9	8:21 PM	12:21 AM	5:31 AM	12:50 PM	7	6
FRI 10	9:39 PM	1:19 AM	6:10 AM	1:50 PM	5	5
SAT 11	10:53 PM	2:21 AM	6:58 AM	2:52 PM	4	4

OCTOBER 2025

POPULAR PLACE ADJUSTMENTS (See full list on page 7)

DAY	MINOR BITE	MAJOR BITE	MINOR BITE	MAJOR BITE	SALT WATER RATING	FRESH WATER RATING
SUN 12	11:57 PM	3:25 AM	7:55 AM	3:56 PM	3	6
MON 13		4:28 AM	9:01 AM	4:57 PM	4	4
TUE 14	12:48 AM	5:27 AM	10:11 AM	5:54 PM	5	5
WED 15	1:30 AM	6:22 AM	11:21 AM	6:47 PM	6	6
THUR 16	2:03 AM	7:12 AM	12:29 PM	7:34 PM	7	7
FRI 17	2:30 AM	7:58 AM	1:34 PM	8:18 PM	7	8
SAT 18	2:54 AM	8:40 AM	2:35 PM	9:00 PM	5	8
SUN 19	3:16 AM	9:21 AM	3:36 PM	9:41 PM	6	7
MON 20	3:37 AM	10:01 AM	4:35 PM	10:21 PM	8	8
TUE 21	3:59 AM	10:42 AM	5:35 PM	11:03 PM	● 8	8
WED 22	4:23 AM	11:24 AM	6:35 PM	11:45 PM	8	8
THUR 23	4:49 AM	12:08 PM	7:36 PM		8	6
FRI 24	5:20 AM	12:55 PM	8:37 PM	12:31 AM	7	6
SAT 25	5:57 AM	1:44 PM	9:36 PM	1:19 AM	6	7
SUN 26	6:41 AM	2:35 PM	10:31 PM	2:09 AM	5	5
MON 27	7:32 AM	3:27 PM	11:19 PM	3:00 AM	4	6
TUE 28	8:30 AM	4:19 PM		3:53 AM	3	5
WED 29	9:33 AM	5:10 PM	12:01 AM	4:44 AM	3	5
THUR 30	10:39 AM	5:59 PM	12:37 AM	5:34 AM	4	6
FRI 31	11:46 AM	6:47 PM	1:08 AM	6:23 AM	5	6

Apogee moon phase on Thursday 20th
Perigee moon phase on Thursday 6th
● New moon on Thursday 20th
First quarter moon on Friday 28th
○ Full moon on Thursday 6th
Last quarter moon phase on Wednesday 12th

Perth, WA: Rise: 05:00am Set: 06:50pm

(Note: These sun rise/set times are averages for the month)

DAY	MINOR BITE	MAJOR BITE	MINOR BITE	MAJOR BITE	SALT WATER RATING	FRESH WATER RATING
SAT 1	12:54 PM	7:34 PM	1:36 AM	7:10 AM	4	5
SUN 2	2:04 PM	8:21 PM	2:02 AM	7:57 AM	3	5
MON 3	3:16 PM	9:11 PM	2:28 AM	8:46 AM	6	6
TUE 4	4:31 PM	10:03 PM	2:55 AM	9:37 AM	3	8
WED 5	5:50 PM	11:00 PM	3:25 AM	10:31 AM	5	7
THUR 6	7:12 PM		4:01 AM	11:31 AM	○ 7	6
FRI 7	8:31 PM	12:02 AM	4:46 AM	12:34 PM	7	6
SAT 8	9:42 PM	1:07 AM	5:41 AM	1:39 PM	5	5
SUN 9	10:41 PM	2:13 AM	6:46 AM	2:45 PM	4	4
MON 10	11:27 PM	3:17 AM	7:57 AM	3:46 PM	3	6
TUE 11		4:16 AM	9:10 AM	4:41 PM	4	4

NOVEMBER 2025

POPULAR PLACE ADJUSTMENTS (See full list on page 7)

DAY	MINOR BITE	MAJOR BITE	MINOR BITE	MAJOR BITE	SALT WATER RATING	FRESH WATER RATING
WED 12	12:04 AM	5:08 AM	10:20 AM	5:32 PM	5	5
THUR 13	12:33 AM	5:56 AM	11:27 AM	6:18 PM	6	6
FRI 14	12:59 AM	6:40 AM	12:29 PM	7:00 PM	7	7
SAT 15	1:21 AM	7:21 AM	1:30 PM	7:41 PM	7	7
SUN 16	1:42 AM	8:01 AM	2:29 PM	8:21 PM	7	8
MON 17	2:04 AM	8:41 AM	3:28 PM	9:01 PM	5	8
TUE 18	2:27 AM	9:22 AM	4:28 PM	9:44 PM	6	7
WED 19	2:53 AM	10:06 AM	5:29 PM	10:29 PM	8	8
THUR 20	3:22 AM	10:52 AM	6:30 PM	11:15 PM	● 8	8
FRI 21	3:57 AM	11:40 AM	7:29 PM		8	6
SAT 22	4:39 AM	12:31 PM	8:25 PM	12:05 AM	7	6
SUN 23	5:28 AM	1:23 PM	9:16 PM	12:57 AM	7	6
MON 24	6:24 AM	2:15 PM	10:00 PM	1:49 AM	6	7
TUE 25	7:25 AM	3:05 PM	10:37 PM	2:39 AM	5	5
WED 26	8:29 AM	3:54 PM	11:09 PM	3:29 AM	4	6
THUR 27	9:34 AM	4:41 PM	11:37 PM	4:17 AM	3	5
FRI 28	10:39 AM	5:26 PM		5:03 AM	4	6
SAT 29	11:46 AM	6:12 PM	12:02 AM	5:48 AM	5	6
SUN 30	12:54 PM	6:58 PM	12:27 AM	6:34 AM	4	5

Apogee moon phase on Wednesday 17th
Perigee moon phase on Thursday 4th
● New moon on Saturday 20th
First quarter moon on Sunday 28th
○ Full moon on Friday 5th
Last quarter moon phase on Friday 12th

Perth, WA: Rise: 05:00am Set: 07:10pm
(Note: These sun rise/set times are averages for the month)

DAY	MINOR BITE	MAJOR BITE	MINOR BITE	MAJOR BITE	SALT WATER RATING	FRESH WATER RATING
MON 1	2:04 PM	7:47 PM	12:52 AM	7:22 AM	3	5
TUE 2	3:19 PM	8:40 PM	1:20 AM	8:13 AM	6	6
WED 3	4:38 PM	9:39 PM	1:52 AM	9:09 AM	5	7
THUR 4	5:59 PM	10:43 PM	2:31 AM	10:11 AM	3	8
FRI 5	7:16 PM	11:50 PM	3:21 AM	11:16 AM	○ 5	7
SAT 6	8:23 PM		4:22 AM	12:23 PM	7	6
SUN 7	9:17 PM	12:57 AM	5:33 AM	1:28 PM	7	6
MON 8	10:00 PM	2:00 AM	6:49 AM	2:28 PM	5	5
TUE 9	10:33 PM	2:58 AM	8:03 AM	3:23 PM	4	4
WED 10	11:01 PM	3:49 AM	9:13 AM	4:12 PM	3	6
THUR 11	11:25 PM	4:36 AM	10:19 AM	4:57 PM	4	4

POPULAR PLACE ADJUSTMENTS (See full list on page 7)

DAY	MINOR BITE	MAJOR BITE	MINOR BITE	MAJOR BITE	SALT WATER RATING	FRESH WATER RATING
FRI 12	11:47 PM	5:19 AM	11:22 AM	5:39 PM	5	5
SAT 13		6:00 AM	12:22 PM	6:19 PM	6	6
SUN 14	12:08 AM	6:40 AM	1:21 PM	7:00 PM	7	7
MON 15	12:31 AM	7:21 AM	2:21 PM	7:42 PM	7	8
TUE 16	12:56 AM	8:04 AM	3:21 PM	8:26 PM	5	8
WED 17	1:24 AM	8:49 AM	4:22 PM	9:12 PM	5	8
THUR 18	1:57 AM	9:36 AM	5:22 PM	10:01 PM	6	7
FRI 19	2:37 AM	10:27 AM	6:20 PM	10:52 PM	8	8
SAT 20	3:24 AM	11:19 AM	7:13 PM	11:45 PM	● 8	8
SUN 21	4:19 AM	12:11 PM	7:59 PM		8	6
MON 22	5:19 AM	1:02 PM	8:38 PM	12:36 AM	7	6
TUE 23	6:22 AM	1:52 PM	9:11 PM	1:26 AM	6	7
WED 24	7:27 AM	2:39 PM	9:40 PM	2:15 AM	5	5
THUR 25	8:32 AM	3:24 PM	10:06 PM	3:01 AM	4	6
FRI 26	9:37 AM	4:09 PM	10:30 PM	3:46 AM	4	6
SAT 27	10:42 AM	4:53 PM	10:54 PM	4:30 AM	3	5
SUN 28	11:49 AM	5:39 PM	11:19 PM	5:15 AM	4	6
MON 29	12:59 PM	6:28 PM	11:48 PM	6:03 AM	5	6
TUE 30	2:14 PM	7:22 PM		6:55 AM	4	5
WED 31	3:31 PM	8:21 PM	12:23 AM	7:51 AM	3	5

Apogee moon phase on Wednesday 14th
Perigee moon phase on Friday 2nd and Friday 30th
● **New moon on Monday 19th**
First quarter moon on Monday 26th
○ **Full moon on Saturday 3rd**
Last quarter moon phase on Sunday 11th

Perth, WA: Rise: 05:20am Set: 07:20pm

(Note: These sun rise/set times are averages for the month)

DAY	MINOR BITE	MAJOR BITE	MINOR BITE	MAJOR BITE	SALT WATER RATING	FRESH WATER RATING
THUR 1	4:48 PM	9:26 PM	1:06 AM	8:53 AM	5	7
FRI 2	6:00 PM	10:32 PM	2:00 AM	9:58 AM	3	8
SAT 3	7:01 PM	11:38 PM	3:06 AM	11:05 AM	○ 5	7
SUN 4	7:50 PM		4:20 AM	12:09 PM	7	6
MON 5	8:28 PM	12:40 AM	5:37 AM	1:07 PM	7	6
TUE 6	8:59 PM	1:35 AM	6:51 AM	2:00 PM	5	5
WED 7	9:25 PM	2:26 AM	8:01 AM	2:48 PM	4	4
THUR 8	9:49 PM	3:11 AM	9:07 AM	3:32 PM	3	6
FRI 9	10:11 PM	3:54 AM	10:10 AM	4:15 PM	3	6
SAT 10	10:33 PM	4:36 AM	11:11 AM	4:56 PM	4	4
SUN 11	10:57 PM	5:17 AM	12:12 PM	5:38 PM	5	5

JANUARY 2026

POPULAR PLACE ADJUSTMENTS (See full list on page 7)

DAY	MINOR BITE	MAJOR BITE	MINOR BITE	MAJOR BITE	SALT WATER RATING	FRESH WATER RATING
MON 12	11:24 PM	6:00 AM	1:12 PM	6:22 PM	6	6
TUE 13	11:56 PM	6:44 AM	2:13 PM	7:07 PM	7	7
WED 14		7:31 AM	3:14 PM	7:55 PM	7	8
THUR 15	12:33 AM	8:20 AM	4:12 PM	8:45 PM	5	8
FRI 16	1:18 AM	9:12 AM	5:07 PM	9:38 PM	6	7
SAT 17	2:10 AM	10:05 AM	5:55 PM	10:30 PM	8	8
SUN 18	3:09 AM	10:57 AM	6:37 PM	11:22 PM	8	8
MON 19	4:13 AM	11:48 AM	7:13 PM		● 8	8
TUE 20	5:18 AM	12:36 PM	7:43 PM	12:12 AM	8	6
WED 21	6:24 AM	1:23 PM	8:10 PM	12:59 AM	7	6
THUR 22	7:30 AM	2:08 PM	8:35 PM	1:45 AM	6	7
FRI 23	8:35 AM	2:52 PM	8:58 PM	2:30 AM	5	5
SAT 24	9:41 AM	3:37 PM	9:23 PM	3:14 AM	4	6
SUN 25	10:50 AM	4:24 PM	9:50 PM	4:00 AM	3	5
MON 26	12:01 PM	5:15 PM	10:21 PM	4:49 AM	4	6
TUE 27	1:15 PM	6:10 PM	10:59 PM	5:42 AM	5	6
WED 28	2:30 PM	7:10 PM	11:47 PM	6:40 AM	4	5
THUR 29	3:42 PM	8:14 PM		7:42 AM	3	5
FRI 30	4:46 PM	9:19 PM	12:46 AM	8:46 AM	6	6
SAT 31	5:39 PM	10:21 PM	1:55 AM	9:50 AM	5	7

Apogee moon phase on Wednesday 11th
Perigee moon phase on Wednesday 25th
● New moon on Tuesday 17th
First quarter moon on Tuesday 24th
○ Full moon on Monday 2nd
Last quarter moon phase on Monday 9th

Perth, WA: Rise: 05:50am Set: 07:00pm

(Note: These sun rise/set times are averages for the month)

DAY	MINOR BITE	MAJOR BITE	MINOR BITE	MAJOR BITE	SALT WATER RATING	FRESH WATER RATING
SUN 1	6:21 PM	11:19 PM	3:10 AM	10:50 AM	3	8
MON 2	6:55 PM		4:25 AM	11:45 AM	○ 5	7
TUE 3	7:24 PM	12:12 AM	5:38 AM	12:36 PM	7	6
WED 4	7:49 PM	1:01 AM	6:47 AM	1:23 PM	7	6
THUR 5	8:12 PM	1:46 AM	7:53 AM	2:07 PM	5	5
FRI 6	8:35 PM	2:29 AM	8:56 AM	2:50 PM	4	4
SAT 7	8:58 PM	3:11 AM	9:58 AM	3:32 PM	3	6
SUN 8	9:24 PM	3:54 AM	10:59 AM	4:15 PM	4	4
MON 9	9:54 PM	4:38 AM	12:01 PM	5:00 PM	5	5
TUE 10	10:29 PM	5:24 AM	1:02 PM	5:48 PM	5	5
WED 11	11:11 PM	6:12 AM	2:02 PM	6:37 PM	6	6

POPULAR PLACE ADJUSTMENTS (See full list on page 7)

DAY	MINOR BITE	MAJOR BITE	MINOR BITE	MAJOR BITE	SALT WATER RATING	FRESH WATER RATING
THUR 12		7:03 AM	2:58 PM	7:29 PM	7	7
FRI 13		7:55 AM	3:49 PM	8:21 PM	7	8
SAT 14	12:56 AM	8:48 AM	4:33 PM	9:13 PM	5	8
SUN 15	1:59 AM	9:39 AM	5:11 PM	10:03 PM	6	7
MON 16	3:04 AM	10:29 AM	5:44 PM	10:52 PM	8	8
TUE 17	4:11 AM	11:17 AM	6:12 PM	11:40 PM	● 8	8
WED 18	5:18 AM	12:03 PM	6:38 PM		8	6
THUR 19	6:25 AM	12:49 PM	7:02 PM	12:26 AM	7	6
FRI 20	7:32 AM	1:35 PM	7:27 PM	1:11 AM	6	7
SAT 21	8:41 AM	2:22 PM	7:54 PM	1:58 AM	5	5
SUN 22	9:52 AM	3:12 PM	8:24 PM	2:46 AM	4	6
MON 23	11:05 AM	4:06 PM	8:59 PM	3:38 AM	3	5
TUE 24	12:20 PM	5:04 PM	9:43 PM	4:34 AM	4	6
WED 25	1:32 PM	6:05 PM	10:37 PM	5:34 AM	5	6
THUR 26	2:37 PM	7:08 PM	11:41 PM	6:36 AM	4	5
FRI 27	3:32 PM	8:10 PM		7:39 AM	3	5
SAT 28	4:17 PM	9:08 PM	12:52 AM	8:39 AM	6	6

Apogee moon phase on Tuesday 10th
Perigee moon phase on Sunday 22nd
● New moon on Thursday 19th
First quarter moon on Thursday 26th
○ Full moon on Tuesday 3rd
Last quarter moon phase on Wednesday 11th

Perth, WA: Rise: 06:10am Set: 06:30pm

(Note: These sun rise/set times are averages for the month)

DAY	MINOR BITE	MAJOR BITE	MINOR BITE	MAJOR BITE	SALT WATER RATING	FRESH WATE RATING
SUN 1	4:53 PM	10:02 PM	2:06 AM	9:35 AM	5	7
MON 2	5:23 PM	10:51 PM	3:18 AM	10:26 AM	3	8
TUE 3	5:49 PM	11:37 PM	4:28 AM	11:13 AM	○ 5	7
WED 4	6:13 PM		5:34 AM	11:58 AM	7	6
THUR 5	6:36 PM	12:21 AM	6:39 AM	12:42 PM	7	6
FRI 6	6:59 PM	1:04 AM	7:42 AM	1:24 PM	7	6
SAT 7	7:25 PM	1:46 AM	8:44 AM	2:07 PM	5	5
SUN 8	7:53 PM	2:30 AM	9:46 AM	2:52 PM	4	4
MON 9	8:26 PM	3:16 AM	10:49 AM	3:39 PM	3	6
TUE 10	9:05 PM	4:04 AM	11:50 AM	4:29 PM	4	4
WED 11	9:51 PM	4:54 AM	12:47 PM	5:19 PM	5	5

MARCH 2026

POPULAR PLACE ADJUSTMENTS (See full list on page 7)

DAY	MINOR BITE	MAJOR BITE	MINOR BITE	MAJOR BITE	SALT WATER RATING	FRESH WATER RATING
THUR 12	10:44 PM	5:45 AM	1:40 PM	6:11 PM	6	6
FRI 13	11:43 PM	6:37 AM	2:27 PM	7:03 PM	7	7
SAT 14		7:29 AM	3:07 PM	7:53 PM	7	7
SUN 15	12:47 AM	8:19 AM	3:42 PM	8:43 PM	7	8
MON 16	1:52 AM	9:08 AM	4:12 PM	9:31 PM	5	8
TUE 17	2:59 AM	9:55 AM	4:39 PM	10:18 PM	6	7
WED 18	4:07 AM	10:41 AM	5:04 PM	11:03 PM	8	8
THUR 19	5:15 AM	11:27 AM	5:29 PM	11:51 PM	● 8	8
FRI 20	6:25 AM	12:15 PM	5:55 PM		8	6
SAT 21	7:37 AM	1:06 PM	6:25 PM	12:40 AM	7	6
SUN 22	8:52 AM	2:00 PM	6:59 PM	1:33 AM	6	7
MON 23	10:08 AM	2:58 PM	7:41 PM	2:29 AM	5	5
TUE 24	11:23 AM	3:59 PM	8:33 PM	3:28 AM	4	6
WED 25	12:31 PM	5:02 PM	9:34 PM	4:30 AM	3	5
THUR 26	1:29 PM	6:04 PM	10:43 PM	5:32 AM	4	6
FRI 27	2:16 PM	7:03 PM	11:55 PM	6:33 AM	5	6
SAT 28	2:54 PM	7:57 PM		7:30 AM	4	5
SUN 29	3:26 PM	8:46 PM	1:06 AM	8:21 AM	3	5
MON 30	3:52 PM	9:32 PM	2:15 AM	9:09 AM	6	6
TUE 31	4:16 PM	10:16 PM	3:21 AM	9:54 AM	5	7

Apogee moon phase on Tuesday 7th
Perigee moon phase on Sunday 19th
● New moon on Friday 17th
First quarter moon on Friday 24th
○ Full moon on Thursday 2nd
Last quarter moon phase on Friday 10th

Perth, WA: Rise: 06:30am Set: 05:50pm
(Note: These sun rise/set times are averages for the month)

DAY	MINOR BITE	MAJOR BITE	MINOR BITE	MAJOR BITE	SALT WATER RATING	FRESH WATER RATING
WED 1	4:39 PM	10:58 PM	4:26 AM	10:37 AM	3	8
THUR 2	5:02 PM	11:41 PM	5:28 AM	11:19 AM	○ 5	7
FRI 3	5:26 PM		6:30 AM	12:02 PM	7	6
SAT 4	5:53 PM	12:24 AM	7:33 AM	12:46 PM	7	6
SUN 5	6:25 PM	1:09 AM	8:35 AM	1:33 PM	5	5
MON 6	7:01 PM	1:57 AM	9:37 AM	2:21 PM	5	5
TUE 7	7:44 PM	2:46 AM	10:36 AM	3:11 PM	4	4
WED 8	8:34 PM	3:37 AM	11:31 AM	4:02 PM	3	6
THUR 9	9:30 PM	4:28 AM	12:20 PM	4:53 PM	4	4
FRI 10	10:31 PM	5:20 AM	1:03 PM	5:44 PM	5	5
SAT 11	11:35 PM	6:09 AM	1:39 PM	6:33 PM	6	6

APRIL 2026

POPULAR PLACE ADJUSTMENTS (See full list on page 7)

DAY	MINOR BITE	MAJOR BITE	MINOR BITE	MAJOR BITE	SALT WATER RATING	FRESH WATER RATING
SUN 12		6:58 AM	2:10 PM	7:21 PM	7	7
MON 13	12:40 AM	7:44 AM	2:38 PM	8:07 PM	7	8
TUE 14	1:46 AM	8:30 AM	3:03 PM	8:52 PM	5	8
WED 15	2:53 AM	9:16 AM	3:28 PM	9:39 PM	6	7
THUR 16	4:02 AM	10:03 AM	3:54 PM	10:27 PM	8	8
FRI 17	5:14 AM	10:53 AM	4:22 PM	11:19 PM	● 8	8
SAT 18	6:29 AM	11:47 AM	4:55 PM		8	6
SUN 19	7:47 AM	12:45 PM	5:35 PM	12:16 AM	7	6
MON 20	9:06 AM	1:47 PM	6:25 PM	1:15 AM	6	7
TUE 21	10:19 AM	2:52 PM	7:24 PM	2:19 AM	5	5
WED 22	11:23 AM	3:56 PM	8:33 PM	3:23 AM	4	6
THUR 23	12:14 PM	4:57 PM	9:46 PM	4:26 AM	3	5
FRI 24	12:56 PM	5:53 PM	10:58 PM	5:25 AM	4	6
SAT 25	1:29 PM	6:44 PM		6:18 AM	5	6
SUN 26	1:56 PM	7:31 PM	12:08 AM	7:07 AM	4	5
MON 27	2:21 PM	8:14 PM	1:14 AM	7:52 AM	3	5
TUE 28	2:44 PM	8:57 PM	2:18 AM	8:35 AM	6	6
WED 29	3:06 PM	9:38 PM	3:20 AM	9:17 AM	5	7
THUR 30	3:30 PM	10:21 PM	4:21 AM	9:59 AM	5	7

Apogee moon phase on Tuesday 5th
Perigee moon phase on Sunday 17th
● **New moon on Sunday 17th**
First quarter moon on Saturday 23rd
○ **Full moon on Saturday 2nd and Sunday 31st**
Last quarter moon phase on Sunday 10th

Perth, WA: Rise: 06:50am Set: 05:20pm
(Note: These sun rise/set times are averages for the month)

DAY	MINOR BITE	MAJOR BITE	MINOR BITE	MAJOR BITE	SALT WATER RATING	FRESH WATER RATING
FRI 1	3:56 PM	11:05 PM	5:23 AM	10:43 AM	3	8
SAT 2	4:25 PM	11:52 PM	6:25 AM	11:28 AM	○ 5	7
SUN 3	5:00 PM		7:27 AM	12:16 PM	7	6
MON 4	5:41 PM	12:40 AM	8:27 AM	1:05 PM	7	6
TUE 5	6:28 PM	1:31 AM	9:24 AM	1:56 PM	5	5
WED 6	7:22 PM	2:22 AM	10:15 AM	2:47 PM	4	4
THUR 7	8:21 PM	3:13 AM	10:59 AM	3:37 PM	3	6
FRI 8	9:23 PM	4:03 AM	11:37 AM	4:26 PM	3	6
SAT 9	10:26 PM	4:51 AM	12:09 PM	5:14 PM	4	4
SUN 10	11:30 PM	5:37 AM	12:38 PM	5:59 PM	5	5
MON 11		6:22 AM	1:03 PM	6:44 PM	6	6

MAY 2026

POPULAR PLACE ADJUSTMENTS (See full list on page 7)

DAY	MINOR BITE	MAJOR BITE	MINOR BITE	MAJOR BITE	SALT WATER RATING	FRESH WATER RATING
UE 12	12:34 AM	7:06 AM	1:28 PM	7:29 PM	7	7
VED 13	1:41 AM	7:52 AM	1:52 PM	8:15 PM	7	8
HUR 14	2:49 AM	8:39 AM	2:19 PM	9:04 PM	5	8
RI 15	4:02 AM	9:30 AM	2:49 PM	9:57 PM	6	7
AT 16	5:19 AM	10:26 AM	3:26 PM	10:56 PM	8	8
UN 17	6:39 AM	11:28 AM	4:11 PM		● 8	8
ION 18	7:57 AM	12:33 PM	5:08 PM	12:00 AM	8	6
UE 19	9:07 AM	1:41 PM	6:16 PM	1:07 AM	7	6
VED 20	10:06 AM	2:46 PM	7:30 PM	2:13 AM	6	7
HUR 21	10:53 AM	3:46 PM	8:45 PM	3:15 AM	5	5
RI 22	11:30 AM	4:40 PM	9:58 PM	4:13 AM	3	5
AT 23	12:00 PM	5:28 PM	11:06 PM	5:03 AM	4	6
UN 24	12:25 PM	6:13 PM		5:50 AM	5	6
ION 25	12:49 PM	6:56 PM	12:11 AM	6:34 AM	5	6
TUE 26	1:11 PM	7:38 PM	1:14 AM	7:16 AM	4	5
VED 27	1:34 PM	8:20 PM	2:15 AM	7:59 AM	3	5
THUR 28	1:59 PM	9:03 PM	3:16 AM	8:41 AM	6	6
RI 29	2:28 PM	9:49 PM	4:17 AM	9:26 AM	5	7
AT 30	3:00 PM	10:36 PM	5:19 AM	10:12 AM	3	8
UN 31	3:39 PM	11:26 PM	6:20 AM	11:01 AM	○ 5	7

Apogee moon phase on Monday 1st and Sunday 28th
Perigee moon phase on Monday 15th
● New moon on Monday 15th
First quarter moon on Monday 22nd
○ Full moon on Tuesday 30th
Last quarter moon phase on Monday 8th

Perth, WA: Rise: 07:10am Set: 05:10pm

(Note: These sun rise/set times are averages for the month)

DAY	MINOR BITE	MAJOR BITE	MINOR BITE	MAJOR BITE	SALT WATER RATING	FRESH WATER RATING
MON 1	4:25 PM		7:17 AM	11:51 AM	7	6
TUE 2	5:17 PM	12:17 AM	8:10 AM	12:43 PM	7	6
WED 3	6:14 PM	1:09 AM	8:57 AM	1:33 PM	7	6
THUR 4	7:15 PM	1:59 AM	9:36 AM	2:22 PM	5	5
FRI 5	8:17 PM	2:47 AM	10:10 AM	3:09 PM	4	4
SAT 6	9:20 PM	3:33 AM	10:39 AM	3:55 PM	3	6
SUN 7	10:22 PM	4:18 AM	11:05 AM	4:39 PM	4	4
MON 8	11:26 PM	5:01 AM	11:29 AM	5:22 PM	5	5
TUE 9		5:44 AM	11:53 AM	6:06 PM	6	6
WED 10	12:31 AM	6:29 AM	12:18 PM	6:52 PM	7	7
THUR 11	1:40 AM	7:17 AM	12:45 PM	7:42 PM	7	8

JUNE 2026

POPULAR PLACE ADJUSTMENTS (See full list on page 7)

DAY	MINOR BITE	MAJOR BITE	MINOR BITE	MAJOR BITE	SALT WATER RATING	FRESH WATER RATING
FRI 12	2:52 AM	8:09 AM	1:18 PM	8:37 PM	5	8
SAT 13	4:09 AM	9:07 AM	1:58 PM	9:38 PM	6	7
SUN 14	5:28 AM	10:10 AM	2:49 PM	10:44 PM	8	8
MON 15	6:44 AM	11:18 AM	3:52 PM	11:52 PM	● 8	8
TUE 16	7:49 AM	12:26 PM	5:05 PM		8	6
WED 17	8:43 AM	1:30 PM	6:23 PM	12:58 AM	7	6
THUR 18	9:25 AM	2:28 PM	7:40 PM	1:59 AM	6	7
FRI 19	9:59 AM	3:21 PM	8:52 PM	2:54 AM	5	5
SAT 20	10:27 AM	4:09 PM	10:00 PM	3:45 AM	4	6
SUN 21	10:52 AM	4:54 PM	11:05 PM	4:31 AM	3	5
MON 22	11:15 AM	5:36 PM		5:15 AM	4	6
TUE 23	11:38 AM	6:19 PM	12:08 AM	5:57 AM	5	6
WED 24	12:03 PM	7:02 PM	1:09 AM	6:40 AM	4	5
THUR 25	12:30 PM	7:46 PM	2:11 AM	7:24 AM	3	5
FRI 26	1:01 PM	8:33 PM	3:12 AM	8:09 AM	6	6
SAT 27	1:38 PM	9:22 PM	4:13 AM	8:57 AM	6	6
SUN 28	2:21 PM	10:13 PM	5:12 AM	9:47 AM	5	7
MON 29	3:12 PM	11:05 PM	6:06 AM	10:39 AM	3	8
TUE 30	4:08 PM	11:55 PM	6:55 AM	11:30 AM	○ 5	7

Apogee moon phase on Sunday 26th
Perigee moon phase on Monday 13th
● **New moon on Tuesday 14th**
First quarter moon on Tuesday 21st
○ **Full moon on Thursday 30th**
Last quarter moon phase on Wednesday 8th

Perth, WA: Rise: 07:10am Set: 05:30pm
(Note: These sun rise/set times are averages for the month)

DAY	MINOR BITE	MAJOR BITE	MINOR BITE	MAJOR BITE	SALT WATER RATING	FRESH WATER RATING
WED 1	5:09 PM		7:36 AM	12:20 PM	7	6
THUR 2	6:10 PM	12:45 AM	8:12 AM	1:07 PM	7	6
FRI 3	7:13 PM	1:31 AM	8:42 AM	1:53 PM	5	5
SAT 4	8:15 PM	2:16 AM	9:09 AM	2:37 PM	4	4
SUN 5	9:18 PM	2:59 AM	9:33 AM	3:20 PM	3	6
MON 6	10:21 PM	3:42 AM	9:56 AM	4:03 PM	3	6
TUE 7	11:26 PM	4:25 AM	10:20 AM	4:48 PM	4	4
WED 8		5:11 AM	10:45 AM	5:34 PM	5	5
THUR 9	12:35 AM	5:59 AM	11:15 AM	6:26 PM	6	6
FRI 10	1:48 AM	6:53 AM	11:50 AM	7:22 PM	7	7
SAT 11	3:04 AM	7:52 AM	12:34 PM	8:23 PM	7	8

JULY 2026

POPULAR PLACE ADJUSTMENTS (See full list on page 7)

DAY	MINOR BITE	MAJOR BITE	MINOR BITE	MAJOR BITE	SALT WATER RATING	FRESH WATER RATING
SUN 12	4:19 AM	8:56 AM	1:30 PM	9:29 PM	6	7
MON 13	5:29 AM	10:03 AM	2:38 PM	10:36 PM	8	8
TUE 14	6:29 AM	11:09 AM	3:54 PM	11:40 PM	● 8	8
WED 15	7:16 AM	12:11 PM	5:13 PM		8	6
THUR 16	7:54 AM	1:08 PM	6:30 PM	12:39 AM	7	6
FRI 17	8:26 AM	1:59 PM	7:42 PM	1:33 AM	6	7
SAT 18	8:52 AM	2:46 PM	8:50 PM	2:22 AM	5	5
SUN 19	9:17 AM	3:31 PM	9:55 PM	3:08 AM	4	6
MON 20	9:41 AM	4:14 PM	10:59 PM	3:52 AM	3	5
TUE 21	10:05 AM	4:58 PM		4:35 AM	4	6
WED 22	10:32 AM	5:43 PM	12:01 AM	5:20 AM	5	6
THUR 23	11:02 AM	6:29 PM	1:04 AM	6:05 AM	5	6
FRI 24	11:37 AM	7:18 PM	2:05 AM	6:53 AM	4	5
SAT 25	12:18 PM	8:08 PM	3:05 AM	7:43 AM	3	5
SUN 26	1:06 PM	8:59 PM	4:01 AM	8:33 AM	6	6
MON 27	2:00 PM	9:51 PM	4:52 AM	9:24 AM	5	7
TUE 28	3:00 PM	10:41 PM	5:36 AM	10:16 AM	3	8
WED 29	4:02 PM	11:29 PM	6:13 AM	11:05 AM	5	7
THUR 30	5:05 PM		6:45 AM	11:52 AM	○ 5	7
FRI 31	6:09 PM	12:15 AM	7:13 AM	12:37 PM	7	6

Apogee moon phase on Saturday 22nd
Perigee moon phase on Monday 10th
● **New moon on Thursday 13th**
First quarter moon on Thursday 20th
○ **Full moon on Friday 28th**
Last quarter moon phase on Thursday 6th

Perth, WA: Rise: 06:50am Set: 05:40pm
(Note: These sun rise/set times are averages for the month)

DAY	MINOR BITE	MAJOR BITE	MINOR BITE	MAJOR BITE	SALT WATER RATING	FRESH WATER RATING
SAT 1	7:12 PM	12:59 AM	7:38 AM	1:20 PM	7	6
SUN 2	8:14 PM	1:42 AM	8:02 AM	2:03 PM	5	5
MON 3	9:19 PM	2:25 AM	8:25 AM	2:46 PM	4	4
TUE 4	10:26 PM	3:09 AM	8:49 AM	3:31 PM	3	6
WED 5	11:35 PM	3:55 AM	9:17 AM	4:20 PM	4	4
THUR 6		4:46 AM	9:49 AM	5:13 PM	5	5
FRI 7	12:48 AM	5:41 AM	10:28 AM	6:11 PM	6	6
SAT 8	2:02 AM	6:41 AM	11:17 AM	7:12 PM	7	7
SUN 9	3:12 AM	7:45 AM	12:18 PM	8:17 PM	7	8
MON 10	4:15 AM	8:50 AM	1:29 PM	9:21 PM	5	8
TUE 11	5:07 AM	9:53 AM	2:46 PM	10:22 PM	6	7

AUGUST 2026

POPULAR PLACE ADJUSTMENTS (See full list on page 7)

DAY	MINOR BITE	MAJOR BITE	MINOR BITE	MAJOR BITE	SALT WATER RATING	FRESH WATER RATING
WED 12	5:48 AM	10:52 AM	4:04 PM	11:18 PM	8	8
THUR 13	6:22 AM	11:46 AM	5:18 PM		● 8	8
FRI 14	6:51 AM	12:35 PM	6:29 PM	12:10 AM	8	6
SAT 15	7:17 AM	1:22 PM	7:37 PM	12:58 AM	7	6
SUN 16	7:41 AM	2:07 PM	8:43 PM	1:44 AM	6	7
MON 17	8:06 AM	2:51 PM	9:47 PM	2:29 AM	5	5
TUE 18	8:32 AM	3:36 PM	10:51 PM	3:13 AM	4	6
WED 19	9:01 AM	4:23 PM	11:54 PM	3:59 AM	3	5
THUR 20	9:34 AM	5:11 PM		4:46 AM	4	6
FRI 21	10:13 AM	6:01 PM	12:55 AM	5:35 AM	5	6
SAT 22	10:59 AM	6:52 PM	1:53 AM	6:26 AM	4	5
SUN 23	11:51 AM	7:44 PM	2:46 AM	7:17 AM	3	5
MON 24	12:49 PM	8:34 PM	3:32 AM	8:09 AM	3	5
TUE 25	1:51 PM	9:23 PM	4:12 AM	8:58 AM	6	6
WED 26	2:54 PM	10:10 PM	4:46 AM	9:46 AM	5	7
THUR 27	3:58 PM	10:55 PM	5:16 AM	10:32 AM	3	8
FRI 28	5:02 PM	11:39 PM	5:42 AM	11:16 AM	○ 5	7
SAT 29	6:06 PM		6:06 AM	12:01 PM	7	6
SUN 30	7:11 PM	12:23 AM	6:30 AM	12:45 PM	7	6
MON 31	8:17 PM	1:07 AM	6:54 AM	1:30 PM	5	5

Apogee moon phase on Saturday 19th
Perigee moon phase on Monday 7th
● New moon on Friday 11th
First quarter moon on Saturday 19th
○ Full moon on Sunday 27th
Last quarter moon phase on Friday 4th

Perth, WA: Rise: 06:50am Set: 05:40pm
(Note: These sun rise/set times are averages for the month)

DAY	MINOR BITE	MAJOR BITE	MINOR BITE	MAJOR BITE	SALT WATER RATING	FRESH WATER RATING
TUE 1	9:27 PM	1:53 AM	7:20 AM	2:18 PM	4	4
WED 2	10:39 PM	2:43 AM	7:51 AM	3:09 PM	3	6
THUR 3	11:52 PM	3:37 AM	8:28 AM	4:06 PM	4	4
FRI 4		4:35 AM	9:13 AM	5:05 PM	5	5
SAT 5	1:02 AM	5:36 AM	10:09 AM	6:07 PM	6	6
SUN 6	2:06 AM	6:39 AM	11:15 AM	7:10 PM	7	7
MON 7	3:00 AM	7:41 AM	12:28 PM	8:10 PM	7	8
TUE 8	3:44 AM	8:40 AM	1:43 PM	9:07 PM	5	8
WED 9	4:20 AM	9:34 AM	2:57 PM	9:59 PM	6	7
THUR 10	4:50 AM	10:25 AM	4:08 PM	10:48 PM	8	8
FRI 11	5:17 AM	11:12 AM	5:17 PM	11:34 PM	● 8	8

SEPTEMBER 2026

POPULAR PLACE ADJUSTMENTS (See full list on page 7)

DAY	MINOR BITE	MAJOR BITE	MINOR BITE	MAJOR BITE	SALT WATER RATING	FRESH WATER RATING
SAT 12	5:42 AM	11:58 AM	6:24 PM		8	6
SUN 13	6:07 AM	12:43 PM	7:29 PM	12:20 AM	7	6
MON 14	6:32 AM	1:28 PM	8:34 PM	1:05 AM	6	7
TUE 15	7:00 AM	2:15 PM	9:39 PM	1:51 AM	5	5
WED 16	7:32 AM	3:03 PM	10:42 PM	2:38 AM	5	5
THUR 17	8:09 AM	3:53 PM	11:42 PM	3:28 AM	4	6
FRI 18	8:52 AM	4:44 PM		4:18 AM	3	5
SAT 19	9:42 AM	5:35 PM	12:37 AM	5:09 AM	4	6
SUN 20	10:38 AM	6:26 PM	1:26 AM	6:00 AM	5	6
MON 21	11:37 AM	7:15 PM	2:09 AM	6:50 AM	4	5
TUE 22	12:40 PM	8:03 PM	2:45 AM	7:39 AM	3	5
WED 23	1:43 PM	8:48 PM	3:16 AM	8:25 AM	6	6
THUR 24	2:47 PM	9:33 PM	3:43 AM	9:10 AM	5	7
FRI 25	3:51 PM	10:17 PM	4:08 AM	9:54 AM	3	8
SAT 26	4:57 PM	11:02 PM	4:32 AM	10:39 AM	3	8
SUN 27	6:04 PM	11:48 PM	4:57 AM	11:24 AM	○ 5	7
MON 28	7:14 PM		5:23 AM	12:13 PM	7	6
TUE 29	8:27 PM	12:38 AM	5:53 AM	1:04 PM	7	6
WED 30	9:41 PM	1:31 AM	6:28 AM	2:00 PM	5	5

Apogee moon phase on Saturday 17th
Perigee moon phase on Friday 2nd and Thursday 29th
New moon on Sunday 11th
First quarter moon on Monday 19th
Full moon on Monday 26th
Last quarter moon phase on Saturday 3rd

Perth, WA: Rise: 06:50am Set: 05:40pm

(Note: These sun rise/set times are averages for the month)

DAY	MINOR BITE	MAJOR BITE	MINOR BITE	MAJOR BITE	SALT WATER RATING	FRESH WATER RATING
THUR 1	10:54 PM	2:29 AM	7:11 AM	2:59 PM	4	4
FRI 2		3:30 AM	8:04 AM	4:01 PM	3	6
SAT 3		4:33 AM	9:07 AM	5:03 PM	5	5
SUN 4	12:57 AM	5:35 AM	10:17 AM	6:04 PM	6	6
MON 5	1:43 AM	6:34 AM	11:31 AM	7:00 PM	7	7
TUE 6	2:20 AM	7:28 AM	12:44 PM	7:52 PM	7	7
WED 7	2:52 AM	8:18 AM	1:54 PM	8:41 PM	7	8
THUR 8	3:19 AM	9:06 AM	3:02 PM	9:28 PM	5	8
FRI 9	3:44 AM	9:51 AM	4:08 PM	10:13 PM	6	7
SAT 10	4:08 AM	10:36 AM	5:13 PM	10:57 PM	8	8
SUN 11	4:33 AM	11:20 AM	6:18 PM	11:42 PM	● 8	8

OCTOBER 2026

POPULAR PLACE ADJUSTMENTS (See full list on page 7)

DAY	MINOR BITE	MAJOR BITE	MINOR BITE	MAJOR BITE	SALT WATER RATING	FRESH WATER RATING
MON 12	5:00 AM	12:06 PM	7:23 PM		8	6
TUE 13	5:30 AM	12:54 PM	8:27 PM	12:30 AM	7	6
WED 14	6:05 AM	1:44 PM	9:29 PM	1:19 AM	6	7
THUR 15	6:46 AM	2:35 PM	10:27 PM	2:09 AM	5	5
FRI 16	7:34 AM	3:26 PM	11:19 PM	3:00 AM	4	6
SAT 17	8:27 AM	4:17 PM		3:51 AM	3	5
SUN 18	9:25 AM	5:07 PM	12:03 AM	4:42 AM	3	5
MON 19	10:26 AM	5:55 PM	12:42 AM	5:30 AM	4	6
TUE 20	11:28 AM	6:40 PM	1:14 AM	6:17 AM	5	6
WED 21	12:30 PM	7:25 PM	1:43 AM	7:02 AM	4	5
THUR 22	1:34 PM	8:08 PM	2:08 AM	7:46 AM	3	5
FRI 23	2:38 PM	8:52 PM	2:32 AM	8:30 AM	6	6
SAT 24	3:44 PM	9:38 PM	2:57 AM	9:15 AM	5	7
SUN 25	4:54 PM	10:27 PM	3:22 AM	10:02 AM	3	8
MON 26	6:07 PM	11:20 PM	3:51 AM	10:53 AM	○ 5	7
TUE 27	7:23 PM		4:25 AM	11:48 AM	7	6
WED 28	8:39 PM	12:17 AM	5:06 AM	12:48 PM	7	6
THUR 29	9:50 PM	1:20 AM	5:57 AM	1:52 PM	5	5
FRI 30	10:51 PM	2:24 AM	6:58 AM	2:56 PM	4	4
SAT 31	11:41 PM	3:28 AM	8:08 AM	3:58 PM	3	6

Apogee moon phase on Saturday 14th
Perigee moon phase on Thursday 26th
● New moon on Monday 9th
First quarter moon on Tuesday 17th
○ Full moon on Wednesday 25th
Last quarter moon phase on Monday 2nd

Perth, WA: Rise: 06:50am Set: 05:40pm

(Note: These sun rise/set times are averages for the month)

DAY	MINOR BITE	MAJOR BITE	MINOR BITE	MAJOR BITE	SALT WATER RATING	FRESH WATER RATING
SUN 1		4:29 AM	9:22 AM	4:56 PM	4	4
MON 2	12:22 AM	5:25 AM	10:35 AM	5:50 PM	5	5
TUE 3	12:54 AM	6:16 AM	11:46 AM	6:39 PM	6	6
WED 4	1:23 AM	7:03 AM	12:54 PM	7:25 PM	7	7
THUR 5	1:48 AM	7:48 AM	1:59 PM	8:10 PM	7	8
FRI 6	2:12 AM	8:32 AM	3:03 PM	8:53 PM	5	8
SAT 7	2:36 AM	9:16 AM	4:07 PM	9:38 PM	6	7
SUN 8	3:02 AM	10:01 AM	5:11 PM	10:24 PM	8	8
MON 9	3:31 AM	10:48 AM	6:15 PM	11:12 PM	● 8	8
TUE 10	4:04 AM	11:37 AM	7:17 PM		8	6
WED 11	4:43 AM	12:27 PM	8:17 PM	12:02 AM	7	6

POPULAR PLACE ADJUSTMENTS (See full list on page 7)

DAY	MINOR BITE	MAJOR BITE	MINOR BITE	MAJOR BITE	SALT WATER RATING	FRESH WATER RATING
THUR 12	5:28 AM	1:19 PM	9:11 PM	12:53 AM	7	6
FRI 13	6:19 AM	2:10 PM	9:58 PM	1:44 AM	6	7
SAT 14	7:15 AM	3:00 PM	10:38 PM	2:35 AM	5	5
SUN 15	8:15 AM	3:48 PM	11:13 PM	3:23 AM	4	6
MON 16	9:16 AM	4:34 PM	11:42 PM	4:11 AM	3	5
TUE 17	10:17 AM	5:18 PM		4:56 AM	4	6
WED 18	11:18 AM	6:00 PM	12:08 AM	5:39 AM	5	6
THUR 19	12:20 PM	6:43 PM	12:32 AM	6:21 AM	4	5
FRI 20	1:24 PM	7:27 PM	12:56 AM	7:04 AM	3	5
SAT 21	2:30 PM	8:13 PM	1:20 AM	7:49 AM	6	6
SUN 22	3:41 PM	9:04 PM	1:47 AM	8:38 AM	5	7
MON 23	4:55 PM	9:59 PM	2:18 AM	9:31 AM	5	7
TUE 24	6:13 PM	11:00 PM	2:55 AM	10:29 AM	3	8
WED 25	7:29 PM		3:43 AM	11:33 AM	○ 5	7
THUR 26	8:37 PM	12:06 AM	4:41 AM	12:39 PM	7	6
FRI 27	9:34 PM	1:13 AM	5:51 AM	1:45 PM	5	5
SAT 28	10:19 PM	2:18 AM	7:06 AM	2:47 PM	4	4
SUN 29	10:56 PM	3:17 AM	8:23 AM	3:44 PM	3	6
MON 30	11:26 PM	4:12 AM	9:36 AM	4:36 PM	4	4

Apogee moon phase on Friday 11th
Perigee moon phase on Thursday 24th
● **New moon on Wednesday 9th**
First quarter moon on Thursday 17th
○ **Full moon on Thursday 24th**
Last quarter moon phase on Tuesday 1st and Thursday 31st

Perth, WA: Rise: 06:50am Set: 05:40pm

(Note: These sun rise/set times are averages for the month)

DAY	MINOR BITE	MAJOR BITE	MINOR BITE	MAJOR BITE	SALT WATER RATING	FRESH WATER RATING
TUE 1	11:52 PM	5:01 AM	10:46 AM	5:23 PM	5	5
WED 2		5:47 AM	11:52 AM	6:08 PM	6	6
THUR 3	12:16 AM	6:31 AM	12:57 PM	6:52 PM	7	7
FRI 4	12:40 AM	7:15 AM	2:00 PM	7:37 PM	7	8
SAT 5	1:05 AM	7:59 AM	3:03 PM	8:22 PM	7	8
SUN 6	1:33 AM	8:45 AM	4:06 PM	9:08 PM	5	8
MON 7	2:04 AM	9:32 AM	5:08 PM	9:56 PM	6	7
TUE 8	2:41 AM	10:22 AM	6:09 PM	10:47 PM	8	8
WED 9	3:24 AM	11:13 AM	7:04 PM	11:38 PM	● 8	8
THUR 10	4:13 AM	12:05 PM	7:54 PM		8	6
FRI 11	5:08 AM	12:55 PM	8:37 PM	12:30 AM	7	6

POPULAR PLACE ADJUSTMENTS (See full list on page 7)

DAY	MINOR BITE	MAJOR BITE	MINOR BITE	MAJOR BITE	SALT WATER RATING	FRESH WATER RATING
SAT 12	6:07 AM	1:44 PM	9:13 PM	1:19 AM	6	7
SUN 13	7:07 AM	2:30 PM	9:43 PM	2:07 AM	6	7
MON 14	8:08 AM	3:14 PM	10:10 PM	2:52 AM	5	5
TUE 15	9:08 AM	3:56 PM	10:34 PM	3:35 AM	4	6
WED 16	10:08 AM	4:38 PM	10:57 PM	4:16 AM	3	5
THUR 17	11:09 AM	5:20 PM	11:21 PM	4:59 AM	4	6
FRI 18	12:12 PM	6:03 PM	11:45 PM	5:41 AM	5	6
SAT 19	1:18 PM	6:50 PM		6:26 AM	4	5
SUN 20	2:29 PM	7:41 PM	12:13 AM	7:15 AM	3	5
MON 21	3:43 PM	8:38 PM	12:46 AM	8:09 AM	6	6
TUE 22	4:59 PM	9:41 PM	1:27 AM	9:09 AM	5	7
WED 23	6:12 PM	10:48 PM	2:19 AM	10:14 AM	3	8
THUR 24	7:17 PM	11:56 PM	3:24 AM	11:22 AM	○ 5	7
FRI 25	8:09 PM		4:39 AM	12:28 PM	7	6
SAT 26	8:51 PM	1:00 AM	5:58 AM	1:29 PM	7	6
SUN 27	9:25 PM	1:59 AM	7:16 AM	2:26 PM	5	5
MON 28	9:53 PM	2:53 AM	8:31 AM	3:17 PM	4	4
TUE 29	10:19 PM	3:42 AM	9:41 AM	4:04 PM	3	6
WED 30	10:44 PM	4:28 AM	10:48 AM	4:50 PM	4	4
THUR 31	11:09 PM	5:13 AM	11:52 AM	5:34 PM	5	5

POPULAR TIDE ADJUSTMENTS

Broome	- 58min
Canarvon	- 5min
Dampier	- 25min
Derby	+ 2hr 30min
Karratha	- 15min
Onslow	- 5min
Port Headland	- 33min

Exmouth

Day	Date	Tide 1
Mon	1	3:03 AM (2.09) **H**
Tue	2	3:32 AM (1.95) **H**
Wed	3*	4:34 AM (1.81) **H**
Thu	4	7:29 AM (1.77) **H**
Fri	5	3:04 AM (1.36) L
Sat	6	3:57 AM (1.15) L
Sun	7	4:38 AM (0.92) L
Mon	8 ○	5:16 AM (0.71) L
Tue	9	12:01 AM (2.28) **H**
Wed	10	12:29 AM (2.42) **H**
Thu	11	12:57 AM (2.53) **H**
Fri	12	1:26 AM (2.58) **H**
Sat	13	1:55 AM (2.56) **H**
Sun	14	2:24 AM (2.47) **H**
Mon	15	2:57 AM (2.31) **H**
Tue	16	3:39 AM (2.09) **H**
Wed	17	4:58 AM (1.87) **H**
Thu	18	1:13 AM (1.40) L
Fri	19	3:20 AM (1.20) L
Sat	20	4:12 AM (0.96) L
Sun	21	4:51 AM (0.75) L
Mon	22 ●	5:26 AM (0.59) L
Tue	23	5:59 AM (0.48) L
Wed	24	12:15 AM (2.39) **H**
Thu	25	12:37 AM (2.42) **H**
Fri	26	12:57 AM (2.42) **H**
Sat	27	1:17 AM (2.38) **H**
Sun	28	1:37 AM (2.32) **H**
Mon	29	1:56 AM (2.22) **H**
Tue	30	2:17 AM (2.10) **H**

SEPTEMBER 2025

Tide 2		Tide 3		Tide 4	
9:59 AM	(0.92) L	3:51 PM	(1.53) **H**	8:45 PM	(1.13) L
11:10 AM	(1.06) L	5:13 PM	(1.37) **H**	8:45 PM	(1.27) L
1:54 PM	(1.09) L				
3:35 PM	(0.93) L	10:33 PM	(1.61) **H**		
9:09 AM	(1.92) **H**	4:16 PM	(0.76) L	10:46 PM	(1.78) **H**
10:03 AM	(2.10) **H**	4:47 PM	(0.62) L	11:09 PM	(1.95) **H**
10:47 AM	(2.26) **H**	5:16 PM	(0.52) L	11:35 PM	(2.12) **H**
11:29 AM	(2.35) **H**	5:45 PM	(0.46) **L**		
5:56 AM	(0.52) L	12:09 PM	(2.40) **H**	6:12 PM	(0.45) L
6:35 AM	(0.37) L	12:47 PM	(2.38) **H**	6:40 PM	(0.47) L
7:15 AM	(0.28) L	1:26 PM	(2.31) **H**	7:07 PM	(0.53) L
7:54 AM	(0.28) L	2:03 PM	(2.18) **H**	7:34 PM	(0.62) L
8:33 AM	(0.36) L	2:40 PM	(2.01) **H**	8:00 PM	(0.74) L
9:14 AM	(0.52) L	3:17 PM	(1.81) **H**	8:27 PM	(0.89) L
10:00 AM	(0.73) L	4:02 PM	(1.60) **H**	8:56 PM	(1.07) L
11:12 AM	(0.94) L	5:28 PM	(1.44) **H**	9:35 PM	(1.27) L
1:37 PM	(1.03) L	8:57 PM	(1.50) **H**		
8:00 AM	(1.82) **H**	3:22 PM	(0.91) L	9:57 PM	(1.72) **H**
9:29 AM	(1.98) **H**	4:09 PM	(0.77) L	10:30 PM	(1.93) **H**
10:21 AM	(2.13) **H**	4:43 PM	(0.66) L	11:00 PM	(2.11) **H**
11:03 AM	(2.24) **H**	5:12 PM	(0.59) L	11:28 PM	(2.25) **H**
11:41 AM	(2.28) **H**	5:38 PM	(0.57) L	11:53 PM	(2.34) **H**
12:15 PM	(2.28) **H**	6:02 PM	(0.59) L		
6:29 AM	(0.41) L	12:45 PM	(2.24) **H**	6:25 PM	(0.63) L
6:57 AM	(0.39) L	1:12 PM	(2.18) **H**	6:45 PM	(0.68) L
7:24 AM	(0.40) L	1:36 PM	(2.10) **H**	7:04 PM	(0.74) L
7:49 AM	(0.46) L	2:00 PM	(2.00) **H**	7:23 PM	(0.82) L
8:15 AM	(0.56) L	2:23 PM	(1.88) **H**	7:40 PM	(0.92) L
8:41 AM	(0.70) L	2:48 PM	(1.75) **H**	7:57 PM	(1.03) L
9:14 AM	(0.86) L	3:20 PM	(1.59) **H**	8:14 PM	(1.16) L

Exmouth

POPULAR TIDE ADJUSTMENTS

Broome	- 58min
Canarvon	- 5min
Dampier	- 25min
Derby	+ 2hr 30min
Karratha	- 15min
Onslow	- 5min
Port Headland	- 33min

Day	Date	Tide 1
Wed	1	2:43 AM (1.96) **H**
Thu	2	3:27 AM (1.80) **H**
Fri	3	6:45 AM (1.69) **H**
Sat	4	2:50 AM (1.32) L
Sun	5	3:39 AM (1.05) L
Mon	6	4:20 AM (0.77) L
Tue	7 ○	4:59 AM (0.51) L
Wed	8	5:39 AM (0.30) L
Thu	9	6:18 AM (0.16) L
Fri	10	12:17 AM (2.68) **H**
Sat	11	12:50 AM (2.68) **H**
Sun	12	1:24 AM (2.60) **H**
Mon	13	1:58 AM (2.45) **H**
Tue	14	2:35 AM (2.23) **H**
Wed	15	3:24 AM (1.98) **H**
Thu	16	5:06 AM (1.75) **H**
Fri	17	1:59 AM (1.33) L
Sat	18	3:15 AM (1.10) L
Sun	19	3:59 AM (0.87) L
Mon	20	4:34 AM (0.68) L
Tue	21 ●	5:06 AM (0.53) L
Wed	22	5:37 AM (0.43) L
Thu	23	6:05 AM (0.36) L
Fri	24	6:33 AM (0.34) L
Sat	25	12:18 AM (2.45) **H**
Sun	26	12:42 AM (2.41) **H**
Mon	27	1:05 AM (2.35) **H**
Tue	28	1:29 AM (2.25) **H**
Wed	29	1:54 AM (2.14) **H**
Thu	30	2:25 AM (2.00) **H**
Fri	31	3:18 AM (1.83) **H**

Tide 2		Tide 3		Tide 4	
10:09 AM	(1.03) L	4:29 PM	(1.45) **H**	8:28 PM	(1.31) L
12:31 PM	(1.13) L				
2:41 PM	(1.03) L	9:30 PM	(1.66) **H**		
8:49 AM	(1.84) **H**	3:30 PM	(0.89) L	9:52 PM	(1.87) **H**
9:46 AM	(2.03) **H**	4:03 PM	(0.76) L	10:18 PM	(2.08) **H**
10:32 AM	(2.19) **H**	4:34 PM	(0.67) L	10:46 PM	(2.29) **H**
11:15 AM	(2.28) **H**	5:04 PM	(0.62) L	11:15 PM	(2.46) **H**
11:57 AM	(2.32) **H**	5:35 PM	(0.61) L	11:46 PM	(2.60) **H**
12:37 PM	(2.31) **H**	6:06 PM	(0.62) L		
6:58 AM	(0.12) L	1:15 PM	(2.24) **H**	6:37 PM	(0.67) L
7:38 AM	(0.17) L	1:53 PM	(2.12) **H**	7:07 PM	(0.75) L
8:17 AM	(0.32) L	2:30 PM	(1.98) **H**	7:38 PM	(0.86) L
8:58 AM	(0.53) L	3:09 PM	(1.81) **H**	8:10 PM	(1.01) L
9:45 AM	(0.78) L	4:00 PM	(1.66) **H**	8:50 PM	(1.19) L
10:55 AM	(1.00) L	5:39 PM	(1.57) **H**	10:06 PM	(1.38) L
1:00 PM	(1.10) L	8:04 PM	(1.67) **H**		
8:05 AM	(1.76) **H**	2:35 PM	(1.04) L	9:06 PM	(1.87) **H**
9:19 AM	(1.90) **H**	3:26 PM	(0.94) L	9:44 PM	(2.06) **H**
10:09 AM	(2.03) **H**	4:01 PM	(0.87) L	10:15 PM	(2.22) **H**
10:50 AM	(2.12) **H**	4:31 PM	(0.82) L	10:42 PM	(2.33) **H**
11:26 AM	(2.17) **H**	5:00 PM	(0.80) L	11:07 PM	(2.40) **H**
11:59 AM	(2.18) **H**	5:25 PM	(0.81) L	11:30 PM	(2.44) **H**
12:29 PM	(2.17) **H**	5:49 PM	(0.82) L	11:54 PM	(2.46) **H**
12:55 PM	(2.13) **H**	6:13 PM	(0.85) L		
7:00 AM	(0.37) L	1:20 PM	(2.08) **H**	6:36 PM	(0.89) L
7:28 AM	(0.44) L	1:45 PM	(2.01) **H**	6:58 PM	(0.94) L
7:54 AM	(0.54) L	2:11 PM	(1.93) **H**	7:19 PM	(1.02) L
8:22 AM	(0.68) L	2:40 PM	(1.82) **H**	7:43 PM	(1.12) L
8:55 AM	(0.83) L	3:17 PM	(1.72) **H**	8:10 PM	(1.24) L
9:42 AM	(0.98) L	4:23 PM	(1.63) **H**	8:57 PM	(1.38) L
11:07 AM	(1.11) L	6:27 PM	(1.65) **H**	11:39 PM	(1.46) L

POPULAR TIDE ADJUSTMENTS

Broome	- 58min
Canarvon	- 5min
Dampier	- 25min
Derby	+ 2hr 30min
Karratha	- 15min
Onslow	- 5min
Port Headland	- 33min

Exmouth

Day	Date	Tide 1
Sat	1	5:43 AM (1.70) **H**
Sun	2	2:09 AM (1.26) L
Mon	3*	3:08 AM (0.97) L
Tue	4	3:54 AM (0.68) L
Wed	5	4:37 AM (0.42) L
Thu	6 ○	5:20 AM (0.23) L
Fri	7	6:02 AM (0.13) L
Sat	8	6:45 AM (0.12) L
Sun	9	12:26 AM (2.71) **H**
Mon	10	1:06 AM (2.59) **H**
Tue	11	1:47 AM (2.41) **H**
Wed	12	2:32 AM (2.19) **H**
Thu	13	3:29 AM (1.96) **H**
Fri	14	5:00 AM (1.76) **H**
Sat	15	1:23 AM (1.28) L
Sun	16	2:42 AM (1.09) L
Mon	17	3:30 AM (0.90) L
Tue	18	4:09 AM (0.73) L
Wed	19	4:44 AM (0.59) L
Thu	20 ●	5:15 AM (0.48) L
Fri	21	5:46 AM (0.42) L
Sat	22	6:16 AM (0.40) L
Sun	23	6:47 AM (0.42) L
Mon	24	12:21 AM (2.43) **H**
Tue	25	12:50 AM (2.37) **H**
Wed	26	1:19 AM (2.30) **H**
Thu	27	1:52 AM (2.20) **H**
Fri	28	2:32 AM (2.06) **H**
Sat	29	3:30 AM (1.91) **H**
Sun	30	5:01 AM (1.76) **H**

Tide 2		Tide 3		Tide 4	
1:01 PM	(1.13) L	7:56 PM	(1.81) **H**		
8:06 AM	(1.77) **H**	2:15 PM	(1.07) L	8:43 PM	(2.02) **H**
9:18 AM	(1.92) **H**	3:05 PM	(0.99) L	9:19 PM	(2.24) **H**
10:13 AM	(2.06) **H**	3:45 PM	(0.93) L	9:55 PM	(2.44) **H**
11:01 AM	(2.15) **H**	4:23 PM	(0.88) L	10:30 PM	(2.60) **H**
11:45 AM	(2.20) **H**	5:00 PM	(0.84) L	11:08 PM	(2.71) **H**
12:28 PM	(2.21) **H**	5:37 PM	(0.83) L	11:46 PM	(2.75) **H**
1:08 PM	(2.17) **H**	6:15 PM	(0.85) L		
7:27 AM	(0.21) L	1:47 PM	(2.10) **H**	6:52 PM	(0.90) L
8:08 AM	(0.37) L	2:27 PM	(2.02) **H**	7:31 PM	(0.99) L
8:50 AM	(0.58) L	3:10 PM	(1.93) **H**	8:15 PM	(1.12) L
9:34 AM	(0.79) L	4:02 PM	(1.85) **H**	9:12 PM	(1.26) L
10:29 AM	(0.98) L	5:18 PM	(1.83) **H**	11:00 PM	(1.36) L
11:44 AM	(1.12) L	6:48 PM	(1.89) **H**		
7:16 AM	(1.70) **H**	1:09 PM	(1.18) L	7:57 PM	(2.01) **H**
8:45 AM	(1.77) **H**	2:16 PM	(1.17) L	8:44 PM	(2.14) **H**
9:45 AM	(1.87) **H**	3:06 PM	(1.14) L	9:21 PM	(2.25) **H**
10:32 AM	(1.96) **H**	3:45 PM	(1.10) L	9:53 PM	(2.34) **H**
11:12 AM	(2.02) **H**	4:20 PM	(1.08) L	10:23 PM	(2.40) **H**
11:46 AM	(2.07) **H**	4:52 PM	(1.05) L	10:53 PM	(2.44) **H**
12:17 PM	(2.09) **H**	5:22 PM	(1.03) L	11:22 PM	(2.46) **H**
12:45 PM	(2.09) **H**	5:51 PM	(1.02) L	11:52 PM	(2.46) **H**
1:14 PM	(2.07) **H**	6:19 PM	(1.03) L		
7:17 AM	(0.47) L	1:42 PM	(2.04) **H**	6:47 PM	(1.06) L
7:47 AM	(0.56) L	2:11 PM	(2.00) **H**	7:16 PM	(1.12) L
8:16 AM	(0.66) L	2:43 PM	(1.96) **H**	7:48 PM	(1.19) L
8:48 AM	(0.77) L	3:20 PM	(1.93) **H**	8:30 PM	(1.27) L
9:26 AM	(0.89) L	4:09 PM	(1.91) **H**	9:33 PM	(1.33) L
10:13 AM	(1.01) L	5:12 PM	(1.94) **H**	11:16 PM	(1.32) L
11:17 AM	(1.13) L	6:22 PM	(2.03) **H**		

POPULAR TIDE ADJUSTMENTS

Broome	- 58min
Canarvon	- 5min
Dampier	- 25min
Derby	+ 2hr 30min
Karratha	- 15min
Onslow	- 5min
Port Headland	- 33min

Exmouth

Day	Date	Tide 1
Mon	1	1:06 AM (1.18) L
Tue	2	2:25 AM (0.94) L
Wed	3	3:25 AM (0.68) L
Thu	4	4:17 AM (0.46) L
Fri	5 ○	5:07 AM (0.31) L
Sat	6	5:54 AM (0.23) L
Sun	7	6:40 AM (0.23) L
Mon	8	12:16 AM (2.66) **H**
Tue	9	1:03 AM (2.56) **H**
Wed	10	1:50 AM (2.40) **H**
Thu	11	2:36 AM (2.22) **H**
Fri	12	3:25 AM (2.02) **H**
Sat	13	4:24 AM (1.83) **H**
Sun	14	12:08 AM (1.23) L
Mon	15	1:35 AM (1.15) L
Tue	16	2:45 AM (1.01) L
Wed	17	3:39 AM (0.87) L
Thu	18	4:22 AM (0.73) L
Fri	19	5:00 AM (0.62) L
Sat	20 ●	5:35 AM (0.54) L
Sun	21	6:09 AM (0.50) L
Mon	22	6:42 AM (0.49) L
Tue	23	12:15 AM (2.44) **H**
Wed	24	12:49 AM (2.42) **H**
Thu	25	1:23 AM (2.36) **H**
Fri	26	2:00 AM (2.27) **H**
Sat	27	2:41 AM (2.15) **H**
Sun	28	3:30 AM (2.00) **H**
Mon	29	4:31 AM (1.83) **H**
Tue	30	12:05 AM (1.06) L
Wed	31	1:33 AM (0.95) L

DECEMBER 2025

Tide 2		Tide 3		Tide 4	
7:00 AM	(1.71) **H**	12:35 PM	(1.20) L	7:24 PM	(2.17) **H**
8:38 AM	(1.77) **H**	1:48 PM	(1.22) L	8:17 PM	(2.34) **H**
9:52 AM	(1.87) **H**	2:51 PM	(1.19) L	9:06 PM	(2.50) **H**
10:51 AM	(1.98) **H**	3:45 PM	(1.14) L	9:54 PM	(2.62) **H**
11:41 AM	(2.05) **H**	4:34 PM	(1.07) L	10:42 PM	(2.70) **H**
12:25 PM	(2.11) **H**	5:21 PM	(1.02) L	11:30 PM	(2.71) **H**
1:07 PM	(2.14) **H**	6:07 PM	(0.99) L		
7:23 AM	(0.30) L	1:47 PM	(2.15) **H**	6:52 PM	(0.99) L
8:03 AM	(0.42) L	2:28 PM	(2.15) **H**	7:39 PM	(1.03) L
8:41 AM	(0.58) L	3:07 PM	(2.14) **H**	8:29 PM	(1.10) L
9:15 AM	(0.74) L	3:48 PM	(2.12) **H**	9:26 PM	(1.18) L
9:50 AM	(0.90) L	4:34 PM	(2.11) **H**	10:39 PM	(1.24) L
10:28 AM	(1.06) L	5:26 PM	(2.11) **H**		
5:45 AM	(1.68) **H**	11:18 AM	(1.20) L	6:25 PM	(2.12) **H**
7:30 AM	(1.62) **H**	12:29 PM	(1.31) L	7:24 PM	(2.15) **H**
9:12 AM	(1.67) **H**	1:47 PM	(1.37) L	8:17 PM	(2.19) **H**
10:19 AM	(1.77) **H**	2:54 PM	(1.36) L	9:05 PM	(2.25) **H**
11:05 AM	(1.87) **H**	3:45 PM	(1.32) L	9:47 PM	(2.32) **H**
11:41 AM	(1.95) **H**	4:28 PM	(1.26) L	10:27 PM	(2.37) **H**
12:13 PM	(2.01) **H**	5:04 PM	(1.20) L	11:04 PM	(2.42) **H**
12:43 PM	(2.05) **H**	5:40 PM	(1.15) L	11:40 PM	(2.44) **H**
1:12 PM	(2.09) **H**	6:13 PM	(1.11) L		
7:13 AM	(0.50) L	1:40 PM	(2.11) **H**	6:46 PM	(1.10) L
7:42 AM	(0.54) L	2:09 PM	(2.14) **H**	7:22 PM	(1.11) L
8:10 AM	(0.60) L	2:38 PM	(2.17) **H**	8:00 PM	(1.12) L
8:36 AM	(0.68) L	3:09 PM	(2.19) **H**	8:45 PM	(1.14) L
9:04 AM	(0.79) L	3:42 PM	(2.22) **H**	9:39 PM	(1.14) L
9:35 AM	(0.91) L	4:20 PM	(2.25) **H**	10:46 PM	(1.12) L
10:12 AM	(1.05) L	5:06 PM	(2.28) **H**		
5:55 AM	(1.68) **H**	11:02 AM	(1.21) L	6:06 PM	(2.31) **H**
7:44 AM	(1.62) **H**	12:17 PM	(1.34) L	7:16 PM	(2.36) **H**

POPULAR TIDE ADJUSTMENTS

Broome	- 58min
Canarvon	- 5min
Dampier	- 25min
Derby	+ 2hr 30min
Karratha	- 15min
Onslow	- 5min
Port Headland	- 33min

Exmouth

Day	Date	Tide 1
Thu	1	2:59 AM (0.79) L
Fri	2	4:08 AM (0.62) L
Sat	3 ○	5:04 AM (0.48) L
Sun	4	5:54 AM (0.39) L
Mon	5	6:37 AM (0.36) L
Tue	6	12:20 AM (2.62) **H**
Wed	7	1:07 AM (2.55) **H**
Thu	8	1:50 AM (2.43) **H**
Fri	9	2:30 AM (2.28) **H**
Sat	10	3:06 AM (2.11) **H**
Sun	11	3:44 AM (1.92) **H**
Mon	12	4:29 AM (1.75) **H**
Tue	13	12:00 AM (1.17) L
Wed	14	1:29 AM (1.15) L
Thu	15	3:04 AM (1.05) L
Fri	16	4:09 AM (0.91) L
Sat	17	4:53 AM (0.78) L
Sun	18	5:30 AM (0.67) L
Mon	19 ●	6:02 AM (0.59) L
Tue	20	6:32 AM (0.54) L
Wed	21	12:14 AM (2.48) **H**
Thu	22	12:49 AM (2.48) **H**
Fri	23	1:25 AM (2.44) **H**
Sat	24	2:01 AM (2.36) **H**
Sun	25	2:39 AM (2.24) **H**
Mon	26	3:19 AM (2.07) **H**
Tue	27	4:05 AM (1.87) **H**
Wed	28	5:07 AM (1.67) **H**
Thu	29	12:46 AM (1.03) L
Fri	30	2:47 AM (0.96) L
Sat	31	4:12 AM (0.79) L

Tide 2	Tide 3	Tide 4
9:41 AM (1.69) **H**	1:54 PM (1.39) L	8:28 PM (2.44) **H**
10:53 AM (1.83) **H**	3:18 PM (1.34) L	9:33 PM (2.53) **H**
11:45 AM (1.97) **H**	4:24 PM (1.23) L	10:34 PM (2.60) **H**
12:28 PM (2.09) **H**	5:20 PM (1.12) L	11:30 PM (2.64) **H**
1:06 PM (2.20) **H**	6:10 PM (1.02) L	
7:16 AM (0.38) L	1:43 PM (2.28) **H**	6:58 PM (0.96) L
7:50 AM (0.46) L	2:17 PM (2.34) **H**	7:44 PM (0.95) L
8:20 AM (0.56) L	2:48 PM (2.38) **H**	8:29 PM (0.97) L
8:45 AM (0.69) L	3:17 PM (2.38) **H**	9:13 PM (1.02) L
9:08 AM (0.83) L	3:45 PM (2.36) **H**	9:59 PM (1.08) L
9:30 AM (0.98) L	4:15 PM (2.31) **H**	10:52 PM (1.14) L
9:54 AM (1.14) L	4:52 PM (2.24) **H**	
5:36 AM (1.59) **H**	10:20 AM (1.30) L	5:43 PM (2.16) **H**
7:48 AM (1.51) **H**	11:01 AM (1.47) L	6:57 PM (2.11) **H**
10:40 AM (1.63) **H**	1:45 PM (1.56) L	8:17 PM (2.12) **H**
11:15 AM (1.76) **H**	3:18 PM (1.51) L	9:23 PM (2.20) **H**
11:43 AM (1.89) **H**	4:15 PM (1.40) L	10:15 PM (2.30) **H**
12:09 PM (1.99) **H**	4:57 PM (1.29) L	10:58 PM (2.39) **H**
12:36 PM (2.09) **H**	5:34 PM (1.19) L	11:37 PM (2.45) **H**
1:02 PM (2.17) **H**	6:10 PM (1.10) L	
7:00 AM (0.52) L	1:28 PM (2.26) **H**	6:46 PM (1.03) L
7:26 AM (0.53) L	1:53 PM (2.34) **H**	7:24 PM (0.97) L
7:50 AM (0.57) L	2:17 PM (2.42) **H**	8:02 PM (0.92) L
8:14 AM (0.64) L	2:43 PM (2.47) **H**	8:43 PM (0.90) L
8:37 AM (0.75) L	3:08 PM (2.50) **H**	9:27 PM (0.91) L
9:00 AM (0.88) L	3:37 PM (2.50) **H**	10:16 PM (0.94) L
9:28 AM (1.03) L	4:14 PM (2.46) **H**	11:18 PM (1.00) L
10:00 AM (1.20) L	5:04 PM (2.38) **H**	
6:51 AM (1.53) **H**	10:47 AM (1.38) L	6:24 PM (2.30) **H**
10:01 AM (1.60) **H**	1:06 PM (1.53) L	8:09 PM (2.30) **H**
11:05 AM (1.80) **H**	3:19 PM (1.45) L	9:37 PM (2.40) **H**

POPULAR TIDE ADJUSTMENTS

Broome	- 58min
Canarvon	- 5min
Dampier	- 25min
Derby	+ 2hr 30min
Karratha	- 15min
Onslow	- 5min
Port Headland	- 33min

Exmouth

Day	Date		Tide 1		
Sun	1		5:06 AM	(0.64)	L
Mon	2	○	5:48 AM	(0.53)	L
Tue	3		6:25 AM	(0.47)	L
Wed	4		12:22 AM	(2.59)	**H**
Thu	5		1:04 AM	(2.55)	**H**
Fri	6		1:41 AM	(2.45)	**H**
Sat	7		2:13 AM	(2.32)	**H**
Sun	8		2:42 AM	(2.18)	**H**
Mon	9		3:09 AM	(2.01)	**H**
Tue	10		3:39 AM	(1.85)	**H**
Wed	11		4:15 AM	(1.67)	**H**
Thu	12		5:30 AM	(1.51)	**H**
Fri	13		2:17 AM	(1.22)	L
Sat	14		4:00 AM	(1.08)	L
Sun	15		4:42 AM	(0.92)	L
Mon	16		5:13 AM	(0.78)	L
Tue	17	●	5:42 AM	(0.68)	L
Wed	18		6:08 AM	(0.61)	L
Thu	19		12:08 AM	(2.52)	**H**
Fri	20		12:44 AM	(2.53)	**H**
Sat	21		1:19 AM	(2.49)	**H**
Sun	22		1:55 AM	(2.40)	**H**
Mon	23		2:30 AM	(2.27)	**H**
Tue	24		3:06 AM	(2.09)	**H**
Wed	25		3:44 AM	(1.89)	**H**
Thu	26		4:36 AM	(1.68)	**H**
Fri	27		12:19 AM	(1.14)	L
Sat	28		2:52 AM	(1.10)	L

Tide 2		Tide 3		Tide 4	
11:45 AM	(2.00) **H**	4:32 PM	(1.27) L	10:42 PM	(2.51) **H**
12:20 PM	(2.19) **H**	5:27 PM	(1.08) L	11:35 PM	(2.58) **H**
12:53 PM	(2.34) **H**	6:14 PM	(0.94) L		
6:57 AM	(0.47) L	1:23 PM	(2.46) **H**	6:57 PM	(0.85) L
7:25 AM	(0.52) L	1:50 PM	(2.54) **H**	7:36 PM	(0.80) L
7:48 AM	(0.60) L	2:15 PM	(2.57) **H**	8:12 PM	(0.81) L
8:09 AM	(0.71) L	2:37 PM	(2.57) **H**	8:45 PM	(0.85) L
8:27 AM	(0.82) L	2:58 PM	(2.52) **H**	9:18 PM	(0.92) L
8:44 AM	(0.96) L	3:18 PM	(2.44) **H**	9:54 PM	(1.01) L
8:59 AM	(1.10) L	3:43 PM	(2.33) **H**	10:39 PM	(1.12) L
9:11 AM	(1.26) L	4:14 PM	(2.20) **H**	11:52 PM	(1.22) L
9:04 AM	(1.41) L	5:10 PM	(2.06) **H**		
7:25 PM	(2.00) **H**				
11:34 AM	(1.75) **H**	3:05 PM	(1.62) L	9:10 PM	(2.10) **H**
11:33 AM	(1.90) **H**	4:08 PM	(1.47) L	10:07 PM	(2.25) **H**
11:50 AM	(2.04) **H**	4:49 PM	(1.30) L	10:51 PM	(2.37) **H**
12:12 PM	(2.18) **H**	5:27 PM	(1.14) L	11:30 PM	(2.47) **H**
12:35 PM	(2.32) **H**	6:02 PM	(0.99) L		
6:32 AM	(0.58) L	12:58 PM	(2.45) **H**	6:39 PM	(0.85) L
6:57 AM	(0.59) L	1:21 PM	(2.56) **H**	7:15 PM	(0.74) L
7:20 AM	(0.62) L	1:45 PM	(2.65) **H**	7:52 PM	(0.68) L
7:44 AM	(0.70) L	2:09 PM	(2.70) **H**	8:30 PM	(0.67) L
8:07 AM	(0.80) L	2:33 PM	(2.70) **H**	9:08 PM	(0.73) L
8:30 AM	(0.93) L	3:00 PM	(2.64) **H**	9:51 PM	(0.85) L
8:53 AM	(1.08) L	3:33 PM	(2.52) **H**	10:45 PM	(1.01) L
9:19 AM	(1.25) L	4:20 PM	(2.35) **H**		
6:30 AM	(1.52) **H**	9:45 AM	(1.46) L	5:53 PM	(2.18) **H**
10:26 AM	(1.68) **H**	1:35 PM	(1.62) L	8:28 PM	(2.18) **H**

POPULAR TIDE ADJUSTMENTS

Broome	- 58min
Canarvon	- 5min
Dampier	- 25min
Derby	+ 2hr 30min
Karratha	- 15min
Onslow	- 5min
Port Headland	- 33min

Exmouth

Day	Date	Tide 1
Sun	1	4:08 AM (0.94) L
Mon	2	4:51 AM (0.79) L
Tue	3 ○	5:26 AM (0.68) L
Wed	4	5:57 AM (0.63) L
Thu	5	12:15 AM (2.55) **H**
Fri	6	12:52 AM (2.51) **H**
Sat	7	1:24 AM (2.44) **H**
Sun	8	1:51 AM (2.33) **H**
Mon	9	2:16 AM (2.22) **H**
Tue	10	2:40 AM (2.08) **H**
Wed	11	3:04 AM (1.93) **H**
Thu	12	3:32 AM (1.77) **H**
Fri	13	4:19 AM (1.60) H
Sat	14	12:54 AM (1.33) L
Sun	15	3:21 AM (1.22) L
Mon	16	4:04 AM (1.06) L
Tue	17	4:34 AM (0.93) L
Wed	18	5:01 AM (0.82) L
Thu	19 ●	5:28 AM (0.76) L
Fri	20	5:54 AM (0.73) L
Sat	21	12:32 AM (2.52) **H**
Sun	22	1:09 AM (2.48) **H**
Mon	23	1:45 AM (2.39) **H**
Tue	24	2:19 AM (2.25) **H**
Wed	25	2:55 AM (2.08) **H**
Thu	26	3:33 AM (1.90) **H**
Fri	27	4:30 AM (1.72) **H**
Sat	28	12:11 AM (1.23) L
Sun	29	2:27 AM (1.20) L
Mon	30	3:34 AM (1.08) L
Tue	31	4:15 AM (0.96) L

Tide 2		Tide 3		Tide 4	
10:53 AM	(1.92) **H**	3:43 PM	(1.43) L	9:52 PM	(2.32) **H**
11:23 AM	(2.14) **H**	4:41 PM	(1.19) L	10:48 PM	(2.46) **H**
11:53 AM	(2.34) **H**	5:27 PM	(0.98) L	11:34 PM	(2.54) **H**
12:21 PM	(2.50) **H**	6:06 PM	(0.82) L		
6:25 AM	(0.63) L	12:47 PM	(2.60) **H**	6:43 PM	(0.72) L
6:49 AM	(0.67) L	1:12 PM	(2.67) **H**	7:16 PM	(0.68) L
7:11 AM	(0.73) L	1:32 PM	(2.69) **H**	7:46 PM	(0.68) L
7:30 AM	(0.81) L	1:52 PM	(2.67) **H**	8:15 PM	(0.72) L
7:47 AM	(0.91) L	2:11 PM	(2.61) **H**	8:42 PM	(0.81) L
8:04 AM	(1.02) L	2:30 PM	(2.52) **H**	9:10 PM	(0.93) L
8:19 AM	(1.14) L	2:50 PM	(2.39) **H**	9:45 PM	(1.08) L
8:31 AM	(1.28) L	3:13 PM	(2.25) **H**	10:38 PM	(1.24) L
8:32 AM	(1.42) L	3:46 PM	(2.09) **H**		
6:02 PM	(1.95) **H**				
11:10 AM	(1.79) **H**	2:54 PM	(1.68) L	8:50 PM	(2.04) **H**
10:50 AM	(1.95) **H**	3:54 PM	(1.47) L	9:50 PM	(2.20) **H**
11:04 AM	(2.13) **H**	4:32 PM	(1.25) L	10:35 PM	(2.35) **H**
11:25 AM	(2.31) **H**	5:09 PM	(1.03) L	11:15 PM	(2.45) **H**
11:49 AM	(2.48) **H**	5:45 PM	(0.82) L	11:55 PM	(2.51) **H**
12:14 PM	(2.64) **H**	6:22 PM	(0.65) L		
6:20 AM	(0.73) L	12:39 PM	(2.76) **H**	6:59 PM	(0.54) L
6:46 AM	(0.76) L	1:06 PM	(2.84) **H**	7:36 PM	(0.50) L
7:13 AM	(0.82) L	1:34 PM	(2.85) **H**	8:14 PM	(0.54) L
7:39 AM	(0.92) L	2:02 PM	(2.80) **H**	8:52 PM	(0.67) L
8:04 AM	(1.04) L	2:32 PM	(2.67) **H**	9:33 PM	(0.86) L
8:31 AM	(1.20) L	3:08 PM	(2.48) **H**	10:30 PM	(1.07) L
9:04 AM	(1.38) L	4:00 PM	(2.25) **H**		
7:00 AM	(1.65) **H**	10:07 AM	(1.60) L	6:09 PM	(2.06) **H**
9:24 AM	(1.85) **H**	2:30 PM	(1.57) L	8:43 PM	(2.12) **H**
10:06 AM	(2.09) **H**	3:47 PM	(1.31) L	9:51 PM	(2.27) **H**
10:39 AM	(2.31) **H**	4:33 PM	(1.07) L	10:40 PM	(2.38) **H**

POPULAR TIDE ADJUSTMENTS

Broome	- 58min
Canarvon	- 5min
Dampier	- 25min
Derby	+ 2hr 30min
Karratha	- 15min
Onslow	- 5min
Port Headland	- 33min

Exmouth

Day	Date		Tide 1		
Wed	1		4:48 AM	(0.88)	L
Thu	2	○	5:17 AM	(0.84)	L
Fri	3		12:00 AM	(2.46)	**H**
Sat	4		12:34 AM	(2.43)	**H**
Sun	5		1:03 AM	(2.38)	**H**
Mon	6		1:30 AM	(2.31)	**H**
Tue	7		1:55 AM	(2.22)	**H**
Wed	8		2:18 AM	(2.11)	**H**
Thu	9		2:44 AM	(1.99)	**H**
Fri	10		3:14 AM	(1.86)	**H**
Sat	11		4:05 AM	(1.73)	**H**
Sun	12		6:31 AM	(1.67)	**H**
Mon	13		1:46 AM	(1.32)	L
Tue	14		2:55 AM	(1.21)	L
Wed	15		3:35 AM	(1.10)	L
Thu	16		4:08 AM	(1.01)	L
Fri	17	●	4:39 AM	(0.95)	L
Sat	18		5:11 AM	(0.92)	L
Sun	19		12:17 AM	(2.43)	**H**
Mon	20		12:56 AM	(2.39)	**H**
Tue	21		1:34 AM	(2.32)	**H**
Wed	22		2:12 AM	(2.21)	**H**
Thu	23		2:51 AM	(2.08)	**H**
Fri	24		3:37 AM	(1.95)	**H**
Sat	25		4:45 AM	(1.86)	**H**
Sun	26		6:40 AM	(1.88)	**H**
Mon	27		1:26 AM	(1.26)	L
Tue	28		2:35 AM	(1.21)	L
Wed	29		3:23 AM	(1.14)	L
Thu	30		4:00 AM	(1.09)	L

APRIL 2026

Tide 2		Tide 3		Tide 4	
11:09 AM	(2.48) **H**	5:13 PM	(0.88) L	11:22 PM	(2.45) **H**
11:36 AM	(2.60) **H**	5:48 PM	(0.73) L		
5:45 AM	(0.84) L	12:02 PM	(2.68) **H**	6:21 PM	(0.65) L
6:09 AM	(0.87) L	12:26 PM	(2.72) **H**	6:51 PM	(0.61) L
6:32 AM	(0.91) L	12:48 PM	(2.72) **H**	7:19 PM	(0.62) L
6:54 AM	(0.96) L	1:10 PM	(2.69) **H**	7:45 PM	(0.67) L
7:15 AM	(1.03) L	1:31 PM	(2.63) **H**	8:12 PM	(0.76) L
7:33 AM	(1.12) L	1:52 PM	(2.53) **H**	8:40 PM	(0.90) L
7:51 AM	(1.22) L	2:14 PM	(2.42) **H**	9:11 PM	(1.05) L
8:10 AM	(1.35) L	2:38 PM	(2.28) **H**	9:58 PM	(1.21) L
8:30 AM	(1.49) L	3:14 PM	(2.12) **H**	11:31 PM	(1.33) L
8:54 AM	(1.65) L	4:56 PM	(1.96) **H**		
9:04 AM	(1.83) **H**	2:09 PM	(1.66) L	8:02 PM	(1.98) **H**
9:30 AM	(2.03) **H**	3:19 PM	(1.42) L	9:17 PM	(2.12) **H**
9:58 AM	(2.24) **H**	4:02 PM	(1.15) L	10:09 PM	(2.26) **H**
10:26 AM	(2.44) **H**	4:43 PM	(0.89) L	10:54 PM	(2.36) **H**
10:55 AM	(2.63) **H**	5:21 PM	(0.67) L	11:37 PM	(2.42) **H**
11:25 AM	(2.78) **H**	6:00 PM	(0.50) L		
5:43 AM	(0.91) L	11:58 AM	(2.89) **H**	6:41 PM	(0.41) L
6:15 AM	(0.92) L	12:30 PM	(2.93) **H**	7:20 PM	(0.42) L
6:47 AM	(0.96) L	1:05 PM	(2.90) **H**	8:00 PM	(0.51) L
7:19 AM	(1.04) L	1:41 PM	(2.79) **H**	8:42 PM	(0.68) L
7:54 AM	(1.16) L	2:19 PM	(2.61) **H**	9:27 PM	(0.88) L
8:33 AM	(1.31) L	3:04 PM	(2.39) **H**	10:24 PM	(1.09) L
9:31 AM	(1.48) L	4:12 PM	(2.15) **H**	11:48 PM	(1.23) L
12:00 PM	(1.59) L	6:29 PM	(2.00) **H**		
8:13 AM	(2.04) **H**	2:21 PM	(1.44) L	8:24 PM	(2.05) **H**
9:06 AM	(2.23) **H**	3:26 PM	(1.21) L	9:30 PM	(2.15) **H**
9:45 AM	(2.40) **H**	4:12 PM	(1.00) L	10:21 PM	(2.23) **H**
10:18 AM	(2.53) **H**	4:49 PM	(0.83) L	11:04 PM	(2.28) **H**

Exmouth

POPULAR TIDE ADJUSTMENTS

Broome	- 58min
Canarvon	- 5min
Dampier	- 25min
Derby	+ 2hr 30min
Karratha	- 15min
Onslow	- 5min
Port Headland	- 33min

Day	Date		Tide 1
Fri	1		4:34 AM (1.06) L
Sat	2	○	5:04 AM (1.06) L
Sun	3		12:15 AM (2.30) **H**
Mon	4		12:45 AM (2.28) **H**
Tue	5		1:13 AM (2.23) **H**
Wed	6		1:40 AM (2.18) **H**
Thu	7		2:06 AM (2.11) **H**
Fri	8		2:36 AM (2.03) **H**
Sat	9		3:13 AM (1.95) **H**
Sun	10		4:04 AM (1.89) **H**
Mon	11		5:26 AM (1.88) **H**
Tue	12		12:00 AM (1.29) L
Wed	13		1:19 AM (1.29) L
Thu	14		2:19 AM (1.25) L
Fri	15		3:07 AM (1.19) L
Sat	16		3:50 AM (1.14) L
Sun	17	●	4:30 AM (1.09) L
Mon	18		12:04 AM (2.27) **H**
Tue	19		12:46 AM (2.26) **H**
Wed	20		1:29 AM (2.23) **H**
Thu	21		2:10 AM (2.18) **H**
Fri	22		2:54 AM (2.13) **H**
Sat	23		3:42 AM (2.09) **H**
Sun	24		4:40 AM (2.07) **H**
Mon	25		5:50 AM (2.10) **H**
Tue	26		12:09 AM (1.25) L
Wed	27		1:17 AM (1.29) L
Thu	28		2:18 AM (1.29) L
Fri	29		3:09 AM (1.27) L
Sat	30		3:52 AM (1.24) L
Sun	31	○	4:30 AM (1.21) L

Tide 2		Tide 3		Tide 4	
10:48 AM	(2.61) **H**	5:24 PM	(0.71) L	11:42 PM	(2.31) **H**
11:15 AM	(2.66) **H**	5:56 PM	(0.63) L		
5:33 AM	(1.06) L	11:43 AM	(2.68) **H**	6:26 PM	(0.60) L
6:00 AM	(1.07) L	12:10 PM	(2.68) **H**	6:56 PM	(0.62) L
6:26 AM	(1.09) L	12:36 PM	(2.65) **H**	7:25 PM	(0.67) L
6:50 AM	(1.13) L	1:02 PM	(2.59) **H**	7:53 PM	(0.76) L
7:15 AM	(1.20) L	1:29 PM	(2.51) **H**	8:23 PM	(0.87) L
7:40 AM	(1.28) L	1:56 PM	(2.40) **H**	8:56 PM	(0.99) L
8:10 AM	(1.39) L	2:27 PM	(2.28) **H**	9:37 PM	(1.12) L
8:53 AM	(1.50) L	3:12 PM	(2.13) **H**	10:36 PM	(1.23) L
10:19 AM	(1.60) L	4:37 PM	(1.98) **H**		
6:56 AM	(1.97) **H**	12:57 PM	(1.53) L	6:52 PM	(1.93) **H**
7:59 AM	(2.13) **H**	2:27 PM	(1.31) L	8:29 PM	(1.99) **H**
8:44 AM	(2.33) **H**	3:23 PM	(1.04) L	9:36 PM	(2.10) **H**
9:24 AM	(2.52) **H**	4:11 PM	(0.78) L	10:30 PM	(2.19) **H**
10:03 AM	(2.69) **H**	4:57 PM	(0.57) L	11:19 PM	(2.24) **H**
10:43 AM	(2.82) **H**	5:42 PM	(0.44) L		
5:12 AM	(1.05) L	11:24 AM	(2.89) **H**	6:26 PM	(0.39) L
5:52 AM	(1.03) L	12:07 PM	(2.90) **H**	7:10 PM	(0.42) L
6:33 AM	(1.05) L	12:50 PM	(2.83) **H**	7:54 PM	(0.52) L
7:15 AM	(1.10) L	1:35 PM	(2.70) **H**	8:37 PM	(0.67) L
8:01 AM	(1.18) L	2:22 PM	(2.51) **H**	9:21 PM	(0.84) L
8:55 AM	(1.29) L	3:15 PM	(2.30) **H**	10:08 PM	(1.01) L
10:09 AM	(1.39) L	4:20 PM	(2.10) **H**	11:02 PM	(1.15) L
11:58 AM	(1.41) L	5:57 PM	(1.95) **H**		
7:00 AM	(2.17) **H**	1:38 PM	(1.31) L	7:36 PM	(1.90) **H**
7:58 AM	(2.27) **H**	2:48 PM	(1.14) L	8:55 PM	(1.94) **H**
8:45 AM	(2.37) **H**	3:40 PM	(0.98) L	9:57 PM	(2.00) **H**
9:27 AM	(2.44) **H**	4:22 PM	(0.84) L	10:45 PM	(2.06) **H**
10:03 AM	(2.50) **H**	5:00 PM	(0.73) L	11:27 PM	(2.11) **H**
10:38 AM	(2.54) **H**	5:34 PM	(0.66) L		

POPULAR TIDE ADJUSTMENTS

Broome	- 58min
Canarvon	- 5min
Dampier	- 25min
Derby	+ 2hr 30min
Karratha	- 15min
Onslow	- 5min
Port Headland	- 33min

Exmouth

Day	Date	Tide 1
Mon	1	12:01 AM (2.13) **H**
Tue	2	12:33 AM (2.14) **H**
Wed	3	1:02 AM (2.14) **H**
Thu	4	1:31 AM (2.12) **H**
Fri	5	2:01 AM (2.10) **H**
Sat	6	2:32 AM (2.08) **H**
Sun	7	3:07 AM (2.07) **H**
Mon	8	3:47 AM (2.07) **H**
Tue	9	4:35 AM (2.09) **H**
Wed	10	5:32 AM (2.14) **H**
Thu	11	6:33 AM (2.23) **H**
Fri	12	12:54 AM (1.30) L
Sat	13	2:03 AM (1.30) L
Sun	14	3:05 AM (1.26) L
Mon	15 ●	4:01 AM (1.19) L
Tue	16	4:53 AM (1.11) L
Wed	17	12:43 AM (2.14) **H**
Thu	18	1:26 AM (2.19) **H**
Fri	19	2:07 AM (2.22) **H**
Sat	20	2:48 AM (2.25) **H**
Sun	21	3:28 AM (2.26) **H**
Mon	22	4:09 AM (2.26) **H**
Tue	23	4:53 AM (2.25) **H**
Wed	24	5:43 AM (2.22) **H**
Thu	25	6:40 AM (2.21) **H**
Fri	26	1:00 AM (1.37) L
Sat	27	2:16 AM (1.39) L
Sun	28	3:19 AM (1.35) L
Mon	29	4:08 AM (1.28) L
Tue	30 ○	4:49 AM (1.21) L

Tide 2		Tide 3		Tide 4	
5:05 AM	(1.18) L	11:12 AM	(2.56) **H**	6:08 PM	(0.63) L
5:38 AM	(1.15) L	11:45 AM	(2.57) **H**	6:41 PM	(0.63) L
6:09 AM	(1.14) L	12:17 PM	(2.55) **H**	7:12 PM	(0.66) L
6:39 AM	(1.16) L	12:48 PM	(2.52) **H**	7:43 PM	(0.71) L
7:10 AM	(1.19) L	1:19 PM	(2.45) **H**	8:13 PM	(0.78) L
7:44 AM	(1.24) L	1:52 PM	(2.37) **H**	8:43 PM	(0.86) L
8:22 AM	(1.29) L	2:29 PM	(2.26) **H**	9:15 PM	(0.95) L
9:14 AM	(1.34) L	3:15 PM	(2.12) **H**	9:53 PM	(1.05) L
10:25 AM	(1.36) L	4:21 PM	(1.98) **H**	10:41 PM	(1.15) L
11:58 AM	(1.30) L	5:51 PM	(1.86) **H**	11:43 PM	(1.24) L
1:25 PM	(1.14) L	7:30 PM	(1.83) **H**		
7:32 AM	(2.35) **H**	2:40 PM	(0.93) L	8:59 PM	(1.87) **H**
8:29 AM	(2.49) **H**	3:43 PM	(0.73) L	10:11 PM	(1.95) **H**
9:22 AM	(2.62) **H**	4:38 PM	(0.55) L	11:08 PM	(2.03) **H**
10:15 AM	(2.72) **H**	5:30 PM	(0.44) L	11:58 PM	(2.09) **H**
11:07 AM	(2.77) **H**	6:18 PM	(0.40) L		
5:44 AM	(1.04) L	11:59 AM	(2.77) **H**	7:04 PM	(0.41) L
6:32 AM	(1.01) L	12:48 PM	(2.70) **H**	7:46 PM	(0.48) L
7:22 AM	(1.00) L	1:38 PM	(2.59) **H**	8:26 PM	(0.59) L
8:13 AM	(1.04) L	2:26 PM	(2.43) **H**	9:02 PM	(0.72) L
9:06 AM	(1.09) L	3:14 PM	(2.24) **H**	9:35 PM	(0.87) L
10:06 AM	(1.15) L	4:04 PM	(2.04) **H**	10:10 PM	(1.01) L
11:15 AM	(1.19) L	5:05 PM	(1.86) **H**	10:51 PM	(1.15) L
12:33 PM	(1.18) L	6:26 PM	(1.74) **H**	11:46 PM	(1.28) L
1:52 PM	(1.11) L	8:03 PM	(1.70) **H**		
7:41 AM	(2.21) **H**	3:02 PM	(1.00) L	9:34 PM	(1.75) **H**
8:38 AM	(2.24) **H**	3:58 PM	(0.88) L	10:35 PM	(1.83) **H**
9:30 AM	(2.29) **H**	4:43 PM	(0.77) L	11:18 PM	(1.91) **H**
10:15 AM	(2.35) **H**	5:22 PM	(0.68) L	11:54 PM	(1.97) **H**
10:55 AM	(2.40) **H**	5:57 PM	(0.63) L		

POPULAR TIDE ADJUSTMENTS

Broome	- 58min
Canarvon	- 5min
Dampier	- 25min
Derby	+ 2hr 30min
Karratha	- 15min
Onslow	- 5min
Port Headland	- 33min

Exmouth

Day	Date	Tide 1
Wed	1	12:25 AM (2.02) **H**
Thu	2	12:55 AM (2.06) **H**
Fri	3	1:24 AM (2.10) **H**
Sat	4	1:52 AM (2.13) **H**
Sun	5	2:19 AM (2.17) **H**
Mon	6	2:47 AM (2.21) **H**
Tue	7	3:17 AM (2.24) **H**
Wed	8	3:50 AM (2.26) **H**
Thu	9	4:30 AM (2.27) **H**
Fri	10	5:22 AM (2.27) **H**
Sat	11	6:29 AM (2.29) **H**
Sun	12	1:01 AM (1.34) L
Mon	13	2:36 AM (1.31) L
Tue	14 ●	3:51 AM (1.20) L
Wed	15	4:52 AM (1.06) L
Thu	16	12:37 AM (2.11) **H**
Fri	17	1:15 AM (2.22) **H**
Sat	18	1:52 AM (2.32) **H**
Sun	19	2:26 AM (2.37) **H**
Mon	20	2:57 AM (2.39) **H**
Tue	21	3:26 AM (2.36) **H**
Wed	22	3:56 AM (2.30) **H**
Thu	23	4:30 AM (2.20) **H**
Fri	24	5:16 AM (2.09) **H**
Sat	25	6:27 AM (2.00) **H**
Sun	26	1:18 AM (1.44) L
Mon	27	3:00 AM (1.39) L
Tue	28	4:00 AM (1.27) L
Wed	29	4:43 AM (1.15) L
Thu	30 ○	12:12 AM (1.97) **H**
Fri	31	12:38 AM (2.06) **H**

Tide 2		Tide 3		Tide 4	
5:26 AM	(1.14) L	11:33 AM	(2.44) **H**	6:30 PM	(0.60) L
6:01 AM	(1.09) L	12:09 PM	(2.45) **H**	7:01 PM	(0.59) L
6:35 AM	(1.06) L	12:43 PM	(2.44) **H**	7:30 PM	(0.61) L
7:10 AM	(1.05) L	1:16 PM	(2.40) **H**	7:56 PM	(0.65) L
7:46 AM	(1.04) L	1:51 PM	(2.33) **H**	8:21 PM	(0.70) L
8:27 AM	(1.04) L	2:28 PM	(2.22) **H**	8:47 PM	(0.78) L
9:13 AM	(1.05) L	3:10 PM	(2.09) **H**	9:15 PM	(0.88) L
10:06 AM	(1.05) L	4:00 PM	(1.93) **H**	9:48 PM	(1.00) L
11:12 AM	(1.03) L	5:07 PM	(1.77) **H**	10:30 PM	(1.13) L
12:30 PM	(0.98) L	6:36 PM	(1.64) **H**	11:31 PM	(1.26) L
2:02 PM	(0.88) L	8:29 PM	(1.63) **H**		
7:46 AM	(2.34) **H**	3:28 PM	(0.73) L	10:06 PM	(1.72) **H**
9:01 AM	(2.43) **H**	4:33 PM	(0.58) L	11:07 PM	(1.86) **H**
10:08 AM	(2.53) **H**	5:27 PM	(0.46) L	11:55 PM	(1.99) **H**
11:07 AM	(2.60) **H**	6:13 PM	(0.39) L		
5:45 AM	(0.93) L	12:00 PM	(2.62) **H**	6:53 PM	(0.38) L
6:36 AM	(0.83) L	12:50 PM	(2.58) **H**	7:30 PM	(0.42) L
7:24 AM	(0.78) L	1:36 PM	(2.48) **H**	8:01 PM	(0.50) L
8:10 AM	(0.78) L	2:17 PM	(2.34) **H**	8:30 PM	(0.61) L
8:54 AM	(0.82) L	2:57 PM	(2.16) **H**	8:55 PM	(0.74) L
9:38 AM	(0.88) L	3:34 PM	(1.98) **H**	9:19 PM	(0.88) L
10:25 AM	(0.96) L	4:15 PM	(1.79) **H**	9:45 PM	(1.03) L
11:21 AM	(1.04) L	5:10 PM	(1.62) **H**	10:15 PM	(1.19) L
12:40 PM	(1.08) L	6:45 PM	(1.50) **H**	11:05 PM	(1.35) L
2:23 PM	(1.05) L	9:33 PM	(1.53) **H**		
7:58 AM	(1.99) **H**	3:45 PM	(0.93) L	10:41 PM	(1.66) **H**
9:13 AM	(2.06) **H**	4:35 PM	(0.80) L	11:15 PM	(1.78) **H**
10:06 AM	(2.17) **H**	5:13 PM	(0.68) L	11:44 PM	(1.88) **H**
10:49 AM	(2.27) **H**	5:45 PM	(0.59) L		
5:19 AM	(1.03) L	11:28 AM	(2.34) **H**	6:15 PM	(0.54) L
5:55 AM	(0.94) L	12:03 PM	(2.37) **H**	6:41 PM	(0.51) L

POPULAR TIDE ADJUSTMENTS

Broome	- 58min
Canarvon	- 5min
Dampier	- 25min
Derby	+ 2hr 30min
Karratha	- 15min
Onslow	- 5min
Port Headland	- 33min

Exmouth

Day	Date	Tide 1
Sat	1	1:03 AM (2.14) **H**
Sun	2	1:28 AM (2.22) **H**
Mon	3	1:52 AM (2.29) **H**
Tue	4	2:16 AM (2.34) **H**
Wed	5	2:41 AM (2.37) **H**
Thu	6	3:08 AM (2.36) **H**
Fri	7	3:42 AM (2.31) **H**
Sat	8	4:28 AM (2.23) **H**
Sun	9	5:40 AM (2.14) **H**
Mon	10	12:16 AM (1.36) L
Tue	11	2:43 AM (1.30) L
Wed	12	4:02 AM (1.10) L
Thu	13 ●	5:00 AM (0.89) L
Fri	14	12:17 AM (2.19) **H**
Sat	15	12:51 AM (2.32) **H**
Sun	16	1:22 AM (2.41) **H**
Mon	17	1:50 AM (2.46) **H**
Tue	18	2:15 AM (2.45) **H**
Wed	19	2:38 AM (2.39) **H**
Thu	20	3:00 AM (2.29) **H**
Fri	21	3:26 AM (2.15) **H**
Sat	22	3:58 AM (2.00) **H**
Sun	23	4:56 AM (1.84) **H**
Mon	24	7:24 AM (1.77) **H**
Tue	25	3:02 AM (1.39) L
Wed	26	3:57 AM (1.22) L
Thu	27	4:35 AM (1.04) L
Fri	28 ○	5:10 AM (0.88) L
Sat	29	12:04 AM (2.14) **H**
Sun	30	12:28 AM (2.25) **H**
Mon	31	12:51 AM (2.35) **H**

Tide 2		Tide 3		Tide 4	
6:30 AM	(0.86) L	12:38 PM	(2.38) **H**	7:06 PM	(0.51) L
7:05 AM	(0.79) L	1:12 PM	(2.35) **H**	7:30 PM	(0.53) L
7:41 AM	(0.74) L	1:45 PM	(2.28) **H**	7:52 PM	(0.58) L
8:18 AM	(0.72) L	2:20 PM	(2.18) **H**	8:15 PM	(0.67) L
8:58 AM	(0.72) L	2:58 PM	(2.03) **H**	8:40 PM	(0.77) L
9:41 AM	(0.77) L	3:39 PM	(1.85) **H**	9:06 PM	(0.90) L
10:34 AM	(0.84) L	4:32 PM	(1.66) **H**	9:38 PM	(1.05) L
11:49 AM	(0.91) L	5:56 PM	(1.49) **H**	10:25 PM	(1.22) L
1:45 PM	(0.91) L	8:31 PM	(1.46) **H**		
7:29 AM	(2.11) **H**	3:31 PM	(0.77) L	10:15 PM	(1.63) **H**
9:09 AM	(2.22) **H**	4:33 PM	(0.60) L	11:02 PM	(1.83) **H**
10:18 AM	(2.36) **H**	5:18 PM	(0.47) L	11:42 PM	(2.02) **H**
11:13 AM	(2.46) **H**	5:56 PM	(0.39) L		
5:48 AM	(0.71) L	12:01 PM	(2.50) **H**	6:30 PM	(0.37) L
6:33 AM	(0.59) L	12:45 PM	(2.47) **H**	7:00 PM	(0.41) L
7:15 AM	(0.53) L	1:25 PM	(2.38) **H**	7:28 PM	(0.48) L
7:53 AM	(0.53) L	2:00 PM	(2.25) **H**	7:51 PM	(0.58) L
8:28 AM	(0.57) L	2:31 PM	(2.09) **H**	8:13 PM	(0.69) L
9:01 AM	(0.66) L	3:00 PM	(1.93) **H**	8:31 PM	(0.82) L
9:35 AM	(0.78) L	3:30 PM	(1.75) **H**	8:50 PM	(0.97) L
10:16 AM	(0.92) L	4:06 PM	(1.58) **H**	9:06 PM	(1.12) L
11:21 AM	(1.06) L	5:15 PM	(1.41) **H**	9:15 PM	(1.28) L
1:38 PM	(1.11) L				
3:37 PM	(0.98) L	10:46 PM	(1.59) **H**		
9:09 AM	(1.89) **H**	4:21 PM	(0.83) L	10:58 PM	(1.74) **H**
10:01 AM	(2.04) **H**	4:52 PM	(0.70) L	11:17 PM	(1.88) **H**
10:43 AM	(2.18) **H**	5:19 PM	(0.60) L	11:40 PM	(2.01) **H**
11:19 AM	(2.27) **H**	5:45 PM	(0.53) L		
5:44 AM	(0.73) L	11:54 AM	(2.32) **H**	6:09 PM	(0.50) L
6:18 AM	(0.60) L	12:28 PM	(2.33) **H**	6:32 PM	(0.50) L
6:52 AM	(0.50) L	1:01 PM	(2.31) **H**	6:57 PM	(0.52) L

POPULAR TIDE ADJUSTMENTS

Broome	- 58min
Canarvon	- 5min
Dampier	- 25min
Derby	+ 2hr 30min
Karratha	- 15min
Onslow	- 5min
Port Headland	- 33min

Exmouth

Day	Date	Tide 1
Tue	1	1:15 AM (2.43) **H**
Wed	2	1:39 AM (2.47) **H**
Thu	3	2:04 AM (2.46) **H**
Fri	4	2:30 AM (2.40) **H**
Sat	5	3:02 AM (2.29) **H**
Sun	6	3:46 AM (2.13) **H**
Mon	7	5:12 AM (1.95) **H**
Tue	8	12:55 AM (1.39) L
Wed	9	3:11 AM (1.19) L
Thu	10	4:12 AM (0.92) L
Fri	11 ●	4:59 AM (0.69) L
Sat	12	5:41 AM (0.51) L
Sun	13	12:14 AM (2.43) **H**
Mon	14	12:42 AM (2.49) **H**
Tue	15	1:07 AM (2.50) **H**
Wed	16	1:30 AM (2.46) **H**
Thu	17	1:51 AM (2.38) **H**
Fri	18	2:12 AM (2.26) **H**
Sat	19	2:32 AM (2.12) **H**
Sun	20	2:56 AM (1.96) **H**
Mon	21	3:30 AM (1.78) **H**
Tue	22	6:31 AM (1.65) **H**
Wed	23	3:01 AM (1.37) L
Thu	24	3:45 AM (1.16) L
Fri	25	4:18 AM (0.94) L
Sat	26	4:51 AM (0.73) L
Sun	27 ○	5:25 AM (0.54) L
Mon	28	6:00 AM (0.38) L
Tue	29	12:09 AM (2.50) **H**
Wed	30	12:35 AM (2.56) **H**

Tide 2		Tide 3		Tide 4	
7:27 AM	(0.44) L	1:35 PM	(2.24) **H**	7:20 PM	(0.58) L
8:02 AM	(0.44) L	2:09 PM	(2.13) **H**	7:44 PM	(0.66) L
8:38 AM	(0.49) L	2:43 PM	(1.97) **H**	8:07 PM	(0.77) L
9:17 AM	(0.61) L	3:20 PM	(1.78) **H**	8:31 PM	(0.91) L
10:06 AM	(0.77) L	4:08 PM	(1.58) **H**	9:00 PM	(1.07) L
11:25 AM	(0.94) L	5:40 PM	(1.42) **H**	9:44 PM	(1.25) L
1:52 PM	(0.97) L	9:00 PM	(1.48) **H**		
7:53 AM	(1.93) **H**	3:29 PM	(0.82) L	10:01 PM	(1.71) **H**
9:27 AM	(2.09) **H**	4:17 PM	(0.67) L	10:38 PM	(1.94) **H**
10:25 AM	(2.25) **H**	4:55 PM	(0.55) L	11:12 PM	(2.15) **H**
11:13 AM	(2.35) **H**	5:28 PM	(0.48) L	11:44 PM	(2.32) **H**
11:56 AM	(2.39) **H**	5:58 PM	(0.47) L		
6:19 AM	(0.39) L	12:34 PM	(2.36) **H**	6:25 PM	(0.51) L
6:55 AM	(0.34) L	1:09 PM	(2.28) **H**	6:50 PM	(0.57) L
7:28 AM	(0.36) L	1:39 PM	(2.18) **H**	7:13 PM	(0.65) L
7:57 AM	(0.42) L	2:06 PM	(2.05) **H**	7:32 PM	(0.74) L
8:25 AM	(0.53) L	2:30 PM	(1.92) **H**	7:52 PM	(0.86) L
8:52 AM	(0.68) L	2:55 PM	(1.77) **H**	8:09 PM	(0.98) L
9:25 AM	(0.85) L	3:24 PM	(1.61) **H**	8:24 PM	(1.12) L
10:13 AM	(1.03) L	4:15 PM	(1.45) **H**	8:31 PM	(1.27) L
12:20 PM	(1.16) L				
2:56 PM	(1.08) L	10:07 PM	(1.60) **H**		
8:56 AM	(1.78) **H**	3:43 PM	(0.93) L	10:13 PM	(1.77) **H**
9:47 AM	(1.95) **H**	4:13 PM	(0.80) L	10:30 PM	(1.94) **H**
10:27 AM	(2.10) **H**	4:39 PM	(0.71) L	10:53 PM	(2.11) **H**
11:04 AM	(2.20) **H**	5:04 PM	(0.64) L	11:17 PM	(2.26) **H**
11:40 AM	(2.27) **H**	5:30 PM	(0.61) L	11:43 PM	(2.40) **H**
12:15 PM	(2.29) **H**	5:57 PM	(0.60) L		
6:34 AM	(0.28) L	12:50 PM	(2.26) **H**	6:23 PM	(0.62) L
7:10 AM	(0.24) L	1:24 PM	(2.19) **H**	6:50 PM	(0.67) L

POPULAR TIDE ADJUSTMENTS

Broome	- 58min
Canarvon	- 5min
Dampier	- 25min
Derby	+ 2hr 30min
Karratha	- 15min
Onslow	- 5min
Port Headland	- 33min

Exmouth

Day	Date	Tide 1
Thu	1	1:03 AM (2.57) **H**
Fri	2	1:32 AM (2.52) **H**
Sat	3	2:03 AM (2.40) **H**
Sun	4	2:39 AM (2.23) **H**
Mon	5	3:30 AM (2.01) **H**
Tue	6	5:25 AM (1.81) **H**
Wed	7	1:58 AM (1.31) L
Thu	8	3:18 AM (1.04) L
Fri	9 ●	4:07 AM (0.77) L
Sat	10	4:47 AM (0.56) L
Sun	11	5:25 AM (0.40) L
Mon	12	6:00 AM (0.31) L
Tue	13	6:32 AM (0.28) L
Wed	14	12:24 AM (2.51) **H**
Thu	15	12:48 AM (2.46) **H**
Fri	16	1:12 AM (2.38) **H**
Sat	17	1:35 AM (2.26) **H**
Sun	18	1:58 AM (2.13) **H**
Mon	19	2:23 AM (1.98) **H**
Tue	20	2:57 AM (1.81) **H**
Wed	21	4:53 AM (1.64) **H**
Thu	22	2:20 AM (1.37) L
Fri	23	3:12 AM (1.14) L
Sat	24	3:49 AM (0.89) L
Sun	25 ○	4:25 AM (0.64) L
Mon	26	5:01 AM (0.43) L
Tue	27	5:39 AM (0.27) L
Wed	28	6:16 AM (0.18) L
Thu	29	12:02 AM (2.67) **H**
Fri	30	12:38 AM (2.64) **H**
Sat	31	1:15 AM (2.55) **H**

OCTOBER 2026

Tide 2		Tide 3		Tide 4	
7:45 AM	(0.28) L	1:59 PM	(2.08) **H**	7:17 PM	(0.75) L
8:22 AM	(0.40) L	2:33 PM	(1.93) **H**	7:44 PM	(0.86) L
9:02 AM	(0.58) L	3:12 PM	(1.77) **H**	8:14 PM	(1.00) L
9:52 AM	(0.80) L	4:05 PM	(1.60) **H**	8:51 PM	(1.17) L
11:15 AM	(0.99) L	5:59 PM	(1.51) **H**	10:10 PM	(1.36) L
1:30 PM	(1.04) L	8:23 PM	(1.66) **H**		
8:14 AM	(1.85) **H**	2:55 PM	(0.94) L	9:19 PM	(1.89) **H**
9:28 AM	(2.01) **H**	3:42 PM	(0.82) L	9:58 PM	(2.11) **H**
10:19 AM	(2.15) **H**	4:18 PM	(0.74) L	10:31 PM	(2.30) **H**
11:04 AM	(2.23) **H**	4:51 PM	(0.69) L	11:02 PM	(2.43) **H**
11:44 AM	(2.26) **H**	5:21 PM	(0.68) L	11:31 PM	(2.50) **H**
12:19 PM	(2.25) **H**	5:49 PM	(0.70) L	11:59 PM	(2.53) **H**
12:52 PM	(2.20) **H**	6:15 PM	(0.74) L		
7:01 AM	(0.31) L	1:20 PM	(2.13) **H**	6:39 PM	(0.80) L
7:30 AM	(0.39) L	1:45 PM	(2.04) **H**	7:02 PM	(0.87) L
7:56 AM	(0.50) L	2:10 PM	(1.94) **H**	7:24 PM	(0.96) L
8:23 AM	(0.65) L	2:36 PM	(1.83) **H**	7:45 PM	(1.06) L
8:52 AM	(0.81) L	3:07 PM	(1.71) **H**	8:07 PM	(1.19) L
9:32 AM	(0.99) L	3:58 PM	(1.60) **H**	8:34 PM	(1.33) L
10:49 AM	(1.14) L	6:03 PM	(1.54) **H**	9:45 PM	(1.48) L
1:10 PM	(1.18) L	8:20 PM	(1.67) **H**		
8:05 AM	(1.68) **H**	2:30 PM	(1.10) L	9:00 PM	(1.86) **H**
9:15 AM	(1.83) **H**	3:14 PM	(1.01) L	9:29 PM	(2.05) **H**
10:02 AM	(1.98) **H**	3:47 PM	(0.93) L	9:57 PM	(2.23) **H**
10:45 AM	(2.10) **H**	4:19 PM	(0.86) L	10:27 PM	(2.40) **H**
11:25 AM	(2.17) **H**	4:50 PM	(0.82) L	10:57 PM	(2.53) **H**
12:03 PM	(2.21) **H**	5:22 PM	(0.80) L	11:29 PM	(2.63) **H**
12:40 PM	(2.20) **H**	5:54 PM	(0.80) L		
6:56 AM	(0.18) L	1:16 PM	(2.15) **H**	6:28 PM	(0.83) L
7:35 AM	(0.26) L	1:54 PM	(2.07) **H**	7:01 PM	(0.89) L
8:15 AM	(0.41) L	2:33 PM	(1.97) **H**	7:37 PM	(0.99) L

POPULAR TIDE ADJUSTMENTS

Broome	- 58min
Canarvon	- 5min
Dampier	- 25min
Derby	+ 2hr 30min
Karratha	- 15min
Onslow	- 5min
Port Headland	- 33min

Exmouth

Day	Date	Tide 1
Sun	1	1:54 AM (2.39) **H**
Mon	2	2:40 AM (2.18) **H**
Tue	3	3:44 AM (1.95) **H**
Wed	4	5:42 AM (1.77) **H**
Thu	5	1:48 AM (1.20) L
Fri	6	3:00 AM (0.96) L
Sat	7	3:48 AM (0.74) L
Sun	8	4:30 AM (0.56) L
Mon	9 ●	5:06 AM (0.43) L
Tue	10	5:40 AM (0.36) L
Wed	11	6:12 AM (0.35) L
Thu	12	6:43 AM (0.37) L
Fri	13	12:20 AM (2.44) **H**
Sat	14	12:48 AM (2.37) **H**
Sun	15	1:15 AM (2.28) **H**
Mon	16	1:44 AM (2.17) **H**
Tue	17	2:15 AM (2.04) **H**
Wed	18	2:57 AM (1.89) **H**
Thu	19	4:11 AM (1.73) **H**
Fri	20	12:50 AM (1.34) L
Sat	21	2:15 AM (1.14) L
Sun	22	3:10 AM (0.89) L
Mon	23	3:56 AM (0.64) L
Tue	24	4:39 AM (0.43) L
Wed	25 ○	5:23 AM (0.29) L
Thu	26	6:06 AM (0.22) L
Fri	27	6:49 AM (0.22) L
Sat	28	12:27 AM (2.66) **H**
Sun	29	1:13 AM (2.55) **H**
Mon	30	2:00 AM (2.39) **H**

NOVEMBER 2026

Tide 2		Tide 3		Tide 4	
8:59 AM	(0.61) L	3:17 PM	(1.86) **H**	8:20 PM	(1.11) L
9:47 AM	(0.82) L	4:16 PM	(1.78) **H**	9:21 PM	(1.26) L
10:55 AM	(1.00) L	5:49 PM	(1.78) **H**	11:30 PM	(1.34) L
12:28 PM	(1.10) L	7:23 PM	(1.89) **H**		
7:52 AM	(1.78) **H**	1:51 PM	(1.10) L	8:24 PM	(2.07) **H**
9:09 AM	(1.89) **H**	2:49 PM	(1.05) L	9:09 PM	(2.24) **H**
10:05 AM	(1.99) **H**	3:34 PM	(1.00) L	9:46 PM	(2.37) **H**
10:52 AM	(2.07) **H**	4:12 PM	(0.97) L	10:20 PM	(2.45) **H**
11:32 AM	(2.12) **H**	4:46 PM	(0.95) L	10:52 PM	(2.50) **H**
12:08 PM	(2.13) **H**	5:18 PM	(0.94) L	11:22 PM	(2.50) **H**
12:40 PM	(2.12) **H**	5:48 PM	(0.95) L	11:51 PM	(2.49) **H**
1:08 PM	(2.09) **H**	6:16 PM	(0.97) L		
7:12 AM	(0.44) L	1:35 PM	(2.05) **H**	6:44 PM	(1.01) L
7:40 AM	(0.53) L	2:01 PM	(2.00) **H**	7:11 PM	(1.06) L
8:09 AM	(0.65) L	2:30 PM	(1.94) **H**	7:39 PM	(1.14) L
8:38 AM	(0.77) L	3:03 PM	(1.88) **H**	8:11 PM	(1.24) L
9:12 AM	(0.91) L	3:48 PM	(1.83) **H**	8:57 PM	(1.34) L
9:56 AM	(1.04) L	4:52 PM	(1.81) **H**	10:23 PM	(1.41) L
11:01 AM	(1.16) L	6:15 PM	(1.86) **H**		
6:26 AM	(1.65) **H**	12:30 PM	(1.22) L	7:24 PM	(1.98) **H**
8:16 AM	(1.70) **H**	1:45 PM	(1.22) L	8:15 PM	(2.14) **H**
9:30 AM	(1.82) **H**	2:42 PM	(1.18) L	8:57 PM	(2.31) **H**
10:25 AM	(1.94) **H**	3:29 PM	(1.13) L	9:37 PM	(2.47) **H**
11:12 AM	(2.03) **H**	4:12 PM	(1.07) L	10:17 PM	(2.60) **H**
11:55 AM	(2.09) **H**	4:53 PM	(1.01) L	11:00 PM	(2.68) **H**
12:35 PM	(2.13) **H**	5:35 PM	(0.97) L	11:43 PM	(2.70) **H**
1:15 PM	(2.13) **H**	6:17 PM	(0.96) L		
7:31 AM	(0.30) L	1:55 PM	(2.12) **H**	7:01 PM	(0.98) L
8:14 AM	(0.43) L	2:36 PM	(2.10) **H**	7:48 PM	(1.03) L
8:54 AM	(0.59) L	3:21 PM	(2.09) **H**	8:43 PM	(1.11) L

POPULAR TIDE ADJUSTMENTS

Broome	- 58min
Canarvon	- 5min
Dampier	- 25min
Derby	+ 2hr 30min
Karratha	- 15min
Onslow	- 5min
Port Headland	- 33min

Exmouth

Day	Date		Tide 1
Tue	1		2:52 AM (2.19) **H**
Wed	2		3:52 AM (1.98) **H**
Thu	3		5:14 AM (1.80) **H**
Fri	4		1:03 AM (1.14) L
Sat	5		2:22 AM (0.99) L
Sun	6		3:22 AM (0.83) L
Mon	7		4:09 AM (0.69) L
Tue	8		4:50 AM (0.58) L
Wed	9	●	5:27 AM (0.51) L
Thu	10		6:00 AM (0.47) L
Fri	11		6:33 AM (0.47) L
Sat	12		12:07 AM (2.42) **H**
Sun	13		12:40 AM (2.39) **H**
Mon	14		1:11 AM (2.33) **H**
Tue	15		1:43 AM (2.24) **H**
Wed	16		2:16 AM (2.14) **H**
Thu	17		2:56 AM (2.00) **H**
Fri	18		3:48 AM (1.85) **H**
Sat	19		5:05 AM (1.70) **H**
Sun	20		12:56 AM (1.11) L
Mon	21		2:18 AM (0.94) L
Tue	22		3:27 AM (0.73) L
Wed	23		4:25 AM (0.55) L
Thu	24	○	5:15 AM (0.40) L
Fri	25		6:02 AM (0.32) L
Sat	26		6:46 AM (0.30) L
Sun	27		12:30 AM (2.66) **H**
Mon	28		1:18 AM (2.57) **H**
Tue	29		2:06 AM (2.43) **H**
Wed	30		2:53 AM (2.25) **H**
Thu	31		3:39 AM (2.05) **H**

DECEMBER 2026

Tide 2		Tide 3		Tide 4	
9:34 AM	(0.77) L	4:10 PM	(2.08) **H**	9:51 PM	(1.19) L
10:18 AM	(0.94) L	5:08 PM	(2.09) **H**	11:24 PM	(1.21) L
11:11 AM	(1.09) L	6:13 PM	(2.13) **H**		
6:56 AM	(1.70) **H**	12:18 PM	(1.21) L	7:15 PM	(2.19) **H**
8:31 AM	(1.72) **H**	1:33 PM	(1.26) L	8:11 PM	(2.26) **H**
9:47 AM	(1.80) **H**	2:41 PM	(1.27) L	9:00 PM	(2.33) **H**
10:43 AM	(1.90) **H**	3:34 PM	(1.24) L	9:42 PM	(2.38) **H**
11:27 AM	(1.98) **H**	4:19 PM	(1.20) L	10:21 PM	(2.41) **H**
12:02 PM	(2.03) **H**	4:58 PM	(1.15) L	10:58 PM	(2.43) **H**
12:34 PM	(2.07) **H**	5:33 PM	(1.11) L	11:33 PM	(2.44) **H**
1:03 PM	(2.08) **H**	6:06 PM	(1.09) L		
7:04 AM	(0.50) L	1:30 PM	(2.09) **H**	6:38 PM	(1.09) L
7:32 AM	(0.56) L	1:58 PM	(2.09) **H**	7:09 PM	(1.11) L
8:00 AM	(0.62) L	2:26 PM	(2.09) **H**	7:42 PM	(1.14) L
8:25 AM	(0.71) L	2:55 PM	(2.10) **H**	8:19 PM	(1.19) L
8:51 AM	(0.80) L	3:28 PM	(2.10) **H**	9:05 PM	(1.23) L
9:19 AM	(0.91) L	4:05 PM	(2.11) **H**	10:06 PM	(1.25) L
9:54 AM	(1.04) L	4:50 PM	(2.12) **H**	11:27 PM	(1.22) L
10:39 AM	(1.17) L	5:46 PM	(2.16) **H**		
6:49 AM	(1.62) **H**	11:46 AM	(1.30) L	6:50 PM	(2.23) **H**
8:44 AM	(1.65) **H**	1:14 PM	(1.37) L	7:54 PM	(2.33) **H**
10:10 AM	(1.76) **H**	2:34 PM	(1.35) L	8:54 PM	(2.45) **H**
11:07 AM	(1.89) **H**	3:41 PM	(1.28) L	9:51 PM	(2.57) **H**
11:53 AM	(2.00) **H**	4:37 PM	(1.17) L	10:45 PM	(2.65) **H**
12:35 PM	(2.10) **H**	5:29 PM	(1.07) L	11:38 PM	(2.68) **H**
1:15 PM	(2.19) **H**	6:19 PM	(0.99) L		
7:27 AM	(0.34) L	1:53 PM	(2.27) **H**	7:09 PM	(0.95) L
8:04 AM	(0.43) L	2:30 PM	(2.33) **H**	7:59 PM	(0.94) L
8:38 AM	(0.56) L	3:07 PM	(2.37) **H**	8:51 PM	(0.96) L
9:08 AM	(0.71) L	3:43 PM	(2.38) **H**	9:45 PM	(1.01) L
9:37 AM	(0.87) L	4:19 PM	(2.36) **H**	10:46 PM	(1.07) L

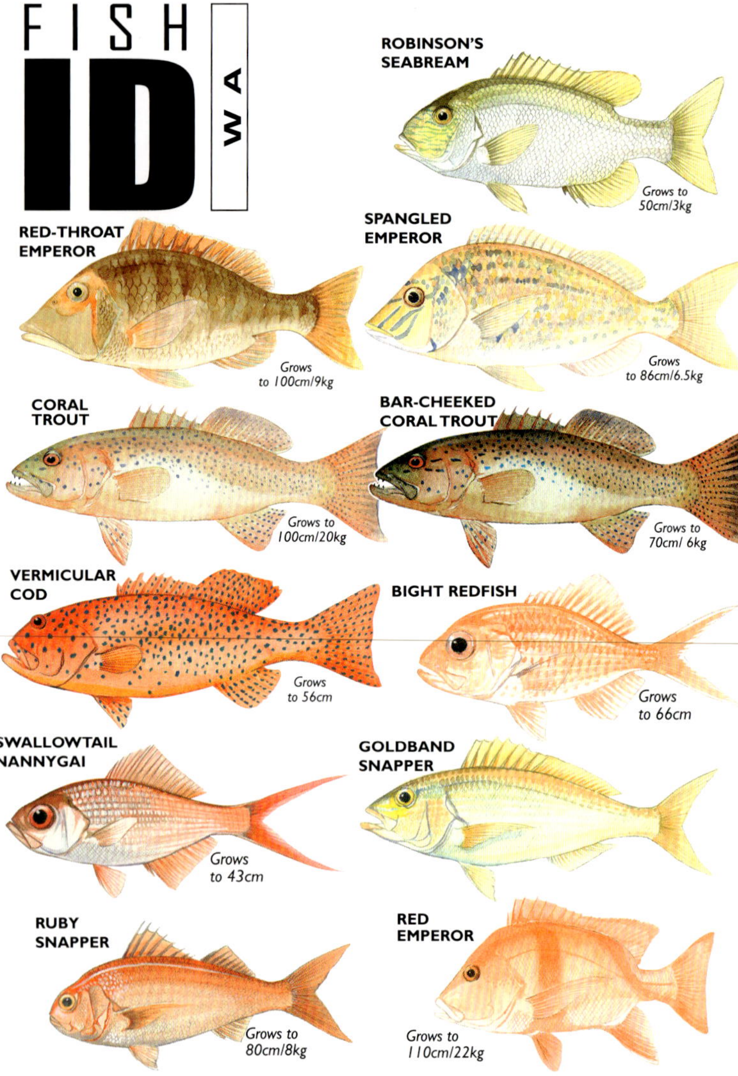
FISH
ID
WA
ROBINSON'S SEABREAM
Grows to 50cm/3kg
RED-THROAT EMPEROR
Grows to 100cm/9kg
SPANGLED EMPEROR
Grows to 86cm/6.5kg
CORAL TROUT
Grows to 100cm/20kg
BAR-CHEEKED CORAL TROUT
Grows to 70cm/ 6kg
VERMICULAR COD
Grows to 56cm
BIGHT REDFISH
Grows to 66cm
SWALLOWTAIL NANNYGAI
Grows to 43cm
GOLDBAND SNAPPER
RUBY SNAPPER
Grows to 80cm/8kg
RED EMPEROR
Grows to 110cm/22kg

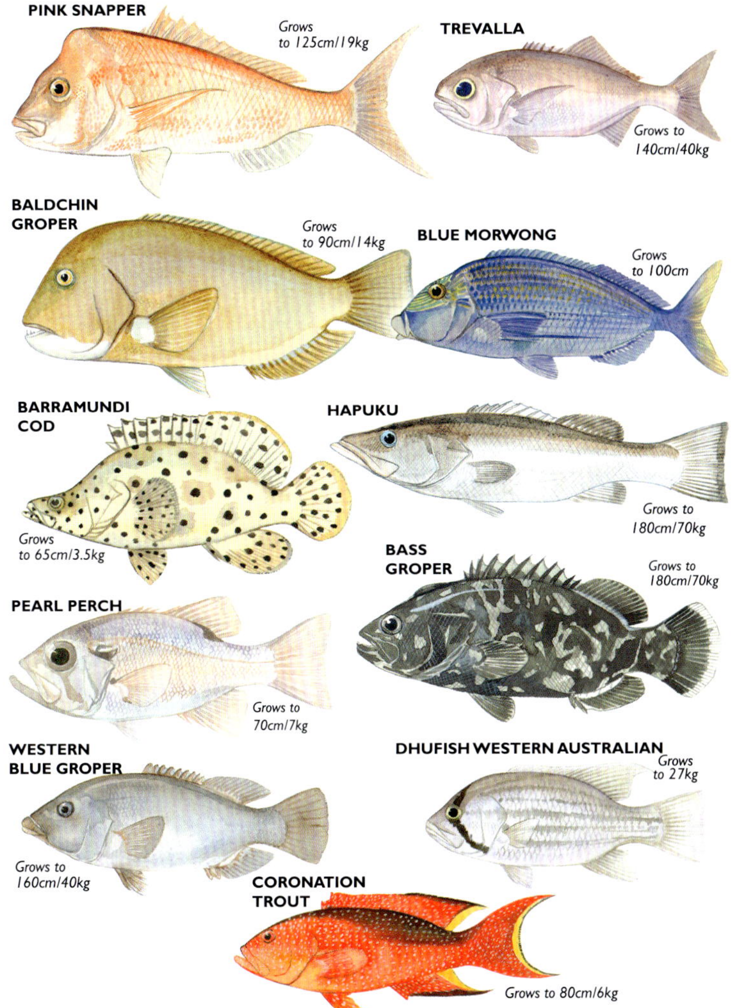
PINK SNAPPER
Grows to 125cm/19kg
TREVALLA
Grows to 140cm/40kg
BALDCHIN GROPER
Grows to 90cm/14kg
BLUE MORWONG
Grows to 100cm
BARRAMUNDI COD
Grows to 65cm/3.5kg
HAPUKU
Grows to 180cm/70kg
BASS GROPER
Grows to 180cm/70kg
PEARL PERCH
Grows to 70cm/7kg
WESTERN BLUE GROPER
Grows to 160cm/40kg
DHUFISH WESTERN AUSTRALIAN
Grows to 27kg
CORONATION TROUT
Grows to 80cm/6kg

SAMSON FISH
YELLOWTAIL KINGFISH
BARRACUDA
Prone to carrying ciguatera
BARRACOUTA
COBIA
WAHOO
SPANISH MACKEREL
SHARK MACKEREL
GREY MACKEREL
MAHI MAHI
GIANT TREVALLY
GOLDEN TREVALLY
MARLIN FAMILY
Pictured: Blue Marlin
SAILFISH
YELLOWFIN TUNA
SOUTHERN BLUEFIN TUNA
DOGTOOTH TUNA
NORTHERN BLUEFIN TUNA
MACKEREL TUNA
STRIPED TUNA

BONITO
Other Tuna
mentioned
ge Pelagics)
CATFISH;
MARINE &
ESTUARY
Poisonous
spines on
pectoral
& dorsal
fins inflict
severe
pain.
BARRAMUNDI
CHINAMAN COD
Grows to 45cm/1.3kg
ACK
EAM
YELLOWFIN
BREAM
DART
FINGERMARK
ATHEAD
tured:
uthern
ue-Spotted Flathead
Pics: Southern
Sand Flathead
FLOUNDER
JAVELIN
FISH
ULLOWAY
BLACK
JEWFISH
SWEETLIPS
LEATHERJACKET
Pictured: Rough
Leatherjacket
ANGROVE
CK
STRIPEY
SEAPERCH
GIANT
THREADFIN
THREADFIN
(OTHER SPECIES)

AUSTRALIAN
HERRING
Grows to
40cm
WHITING
Pictured:
Southern School
Grows to
47cm/1kg
GARFISH
Grows to 50cm
SARDINE,
REDFIN
Grows to
50cm/3kg
BROWN TROUT
Grows to 100cm/14kg
RAINBOW
TROUT
Grows to 80cm/7kg
GRUNTER
Pictured:
Sooty Grunter
Grows to
50cm/4kg
CATFISH
Grows to 85cm/7kg

MUSSELS

OYSTERS

OCTOPUS

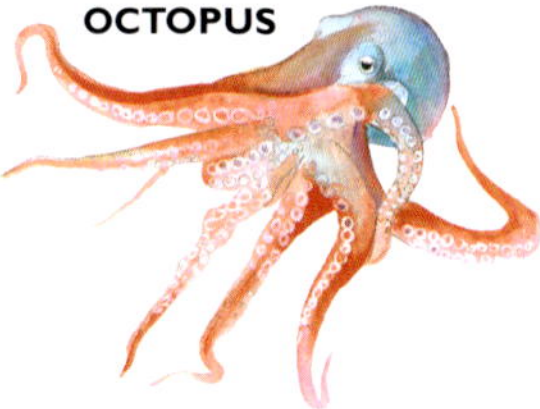

SQUID

CUTTLEFISH

SEA URCHINS

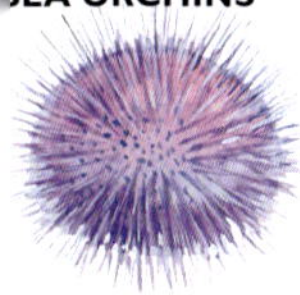

BLOODWORMS

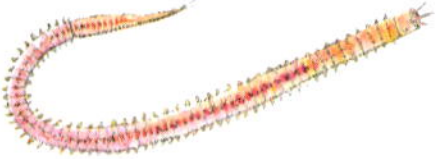

PIPIS

DANGEROUS AND POISONOUS FISH

GIANT TOADFISH

Toxic flesh- never consume

Grows to 97cm

PUFFER FISH

Toxic flesh: never consume

Grows to 15cm

STONEFISH

Extremely dangerous. Avoid contact.

Grows to 47cm

BLACK SPINEFOOT

Poisonous spines inflict severe pain

Grows to 45cm

SMOOTH STINGRAY

Grows to 210cm 340kg

Spines deliver painful wound

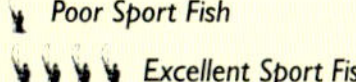

Poor Sport Fish

Excellent Sport Fish

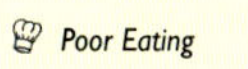

Poor Eating

Excellent Eating

Potentially dangerous

Not to be consumed

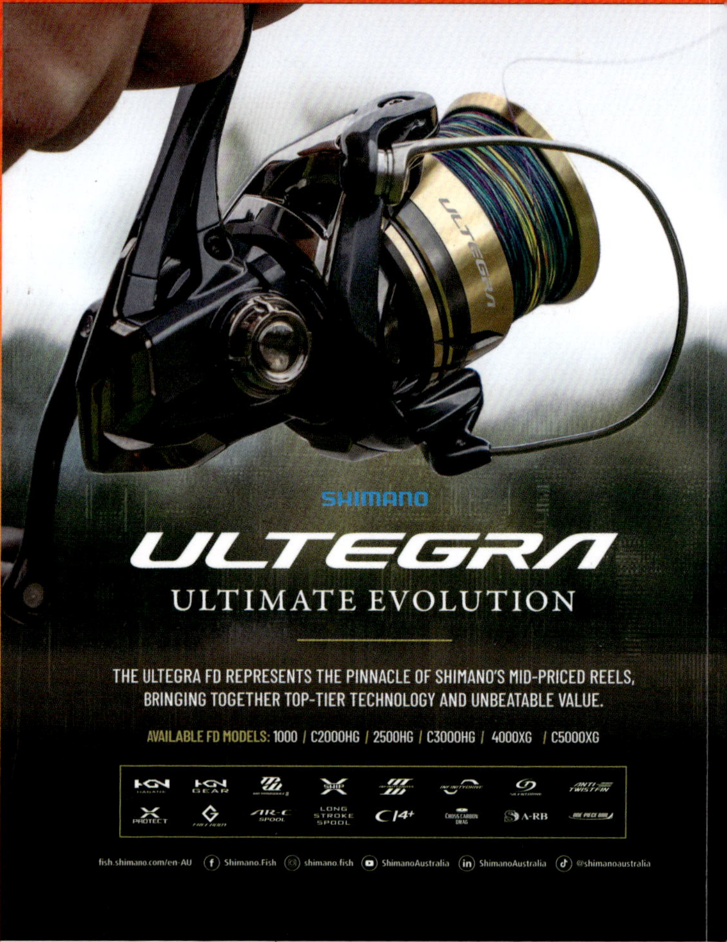

Published by
AFN Fishing & Outdoors
PO Box 544, Croydon, Vic 3136
Tel: (03) 9729 8788
Email: sales@afn.com.au
www.afn.com.au

J1383